Built to Overcome

My Life Defining Moments

Pam Dorsey

B.O.Y. Publications, Inc.
c/o Author Copyrights
P.O. Box 1012
Lowell, NC 28098
www.alwaysbetonyourself.com

PAPERBACK ISBN: 978-1-955605-20-5

Cover and Interior Design: B.O.Y. Enterprises, Inc.

Printed in the United States.

Dedication

I dedicate this book to every woman who thought she was in a storm she would never see her way out of. You can, and you will. I dedicate this book to every woman who will read it and know without a doubt she too is built to overcome.

Acknowledgements

First, foremost and forever I say GOD, Thank You! I would not have been able to complete this assignment without you being with me every step of the way. I Am forever grateful to be Chosen by You! Thank You! I know I Am your favorite …LOL! I love you God, forever and always!

To my husband, my Mr. Wonderful I simply could not do this life without you. You mean the world to me. I Am better than blessed to get to do life with you. Thank you for being the amazing person that you are! God created you perfectly for me! I love you more than words can say; infinity beyond infinity.

To my mommy dearest, my favorite girl, I began this journey when you were still here on earth, and daily you send me the strength to learn how to continue to live without you. Continue to rest well, you earned it, and you deserve it Mommy. Continue to send me your strength. I will always carry you in my heart and I will love you forever girlfriend! You are forever my favorite girl.

Daddy, you have a heart of gold and I know that is one of the many traits of yours that God gifted me with. I love you daddy!

To my handsome heartbeats Javeon and Gavin, I push to create my best life now because I want only the best for both of you. I do this for you! My biggest why comes in the form of each of you. I won't stop, and I can't stop because of the love that I have for you both! I have loved you since your very first heartbeats, and I will love you always!

Carrie, my sissy pooh, my biggest cheerleader and the best intercessor a girl could ask for, you have prayed me through some major storms, and you have become my best friend. I am grateful for our relationship, and I honor our friendship. You are the world's best sister, I love you, my sissy pooh!

Pastor Wendell Jones, your teachings have helped me to become the woman I am today. Many days I walked into your church doors so full I could bust, but your words helped soothe my soul more times that I can count. Your words have helped me to figure out some of my best moves.

Without a doubt you will hear well done thy good and faithful servant! Much love to you!

Melice Jones, when I think of a true, genuine sistahood, I see you. We have weathered some major storms and I wouldn't trade you for the world. Thank you for always being there. You, my dear, are forever my ride or die chica, I love you gurl.

Michelle, our breakfast dates have kept me sane many times, and you had no idea. Thank you for your sincerity and friendship, I love you!

April, my cuzzo! Life separated us, but this book brought us back together. God always has a plan. Thank you for your guidance, your prayers, and mostly your love. I love you cuzzo.

To all of my family and friends near and far, thank you and I love you.

Table of Contents

Preface

What would you tell your younger self? At age 41, I asked myself that question. This book is an account of my life's reflections. Like so many others, I was born to a single mother who worked full time. That alone is a challenging situation. What made matters worse is that my mom was also a functioning alcoholic.

As a child, I found my happy place while riding my bike, roller skating, and visiting family and friends. Those seemed to be the things that kept me sane. Unfortunately, school was not a happy place for me. It was the place where I was bullied, hurt, and humiliated. Without intending it to happen, those experiences began my relationship with low self-esteem and self-sabotage.

By the age of fourteen, living was not my reality. I merely existed. Although I was present, I was often overlooked and unnoticed. Unfortunately, that would be my story for many years to come. At fourteen, I liked nothing about myself or my life. My self-esteem had plunged into the negatives. I began doing things that no teenager should be doing. I continued on my path of self-destruction, self-hate, and self-sabotage for many years.

When I was in my late twenties, I finally acknowledged there was a problem deep within me. I knew I had to face my issues and fix what I believed was wrong with me to improve. My insecurities spawned my sense of low self-worth, and I did not realize the depth of my hurt, nor how to fix it. I made poor choices and bad decisions before I realized I needed healing from the only person who could provide me with what I needed: my Heavenly Father.

I wish that part of my story could be different! Nevertheless, I have learned to own and embrace that part of my life. It has helped to shape me into the woman I am today. Today, I see the importance of breaking cycles and preventing soul ties. I have a greater understanding of how God can turn a negative into a positive and use it for my good, and how the lack of self-love can send a person down the wrong path in life. It has shown me that self-love is the best love to use as the foundation on which I stood to traverse my journey to transformational change.

Life is a journey, not a destination! Allow me to take you on a "COUNTLESS JOURNEY" as I share the teachable moments of truth, hurt, inspiration, and healing through transparency and love. As I learned more about how much God loves me, it helped me to understand my worth and that my value is only found in Him. Learning to love God taught me how to love me! Why? How? Because I am created in His image. If I had not taken my journey of self-love, I wouldn't be able to love others the way God commands. Psalms 139:13-14 is the passage of scripture that began my self-love journey. It taught me that God loves me so much that He formed me, fashioned, covered me and perfectly knitted me in my mother's womb. Now, that's love! When I wasn't aware of how my lack of self-love was hindering my life, God allowed me to hear my Pastor break down these scriptures in ways I had never heard before.

My story reveals how I overcame some tough challenges to encourage others to learn, understand and accept that they too are 'Built to Overcome!'

"These things I have spoken to you, that in Me you may have peace. In the world, you will have tribulation; but be of good cheer, I have overcome the world."
John 16:33 (NIV)

Countless Journey

My middle school years were some of the worst years of my life. I was a loner and extremely shy. I hid under the cover of my dark skin, trying not to bring attention to myself.

I had few friends. There were only a couple of girls that I would hang around at school, and I wasn't a part of the popular crowd by far. They did not consider me the prettiest, or the best dressed. I remember one person who made my middle school years unbearable: Shawn. He was a popular boy and a bully. There wasn't a day that our paths crossed, he didn't make a point of embarrassing me or making me the laughingstock of the school. The impression and impact he left on my life still reverberates in my heart and mind today.

Shawn made me the target of his sadistic torture simply because my skin was darker than his. He called me every derogatory name he could think of. His rude and disheartening words hit my heart like an arrow hitting its target. I cannot describe the emotional and mental pain I experienced that caused my self-esteem to sink lower and lower with each disparaging word. Day in and day out, I endured his offenses. He made my life a living hell.

The harshness flowed out of his mouth so easily. I can never forget his words and the impact they had on my life then and now. Although Shawn said a lot of mean and distasteful things to me, there were a few that seemed to top them all. The one that hurt the most was when he called me a "burnt chocolate chip cookie." He told me that my mother had left me in the oven for too long. I wanted to vanish or disappear just to escape his put-downs. Shawn was an attention monger. He would wait until the bell rang and everyone was in the classroom. Then he would say the meanest things to and about me. He hurled his insults as loud as he could, making sure that everyone heard him, except the teacher, of course!

Shawn's mistreatment and constant barrage of hurtful words had me questioning why I was even born and, more specifically, why I was born with these features and characteristics. What was so wrong with me that this boy thought it was ok, funny even, to treat me this way? There were days when I wished the ground would open and swallow me whole. Just so I would not have to deal with Shawn and his daily antics.

I wished I had two loving and supportive parents at home to help me navigate through the torment and agony of middle school. I am not asking for too much to have one supportive parent who recognized something was wrong; a parent who made me and my emotional/mental health a priority. Unfortunately, that was not my reality.

Like many of my peers, I was raised by a single mother who was a functioning alcoholic. When I say functioning alcoholic, it was because she kept a full-time job. But when she got off work, she spent most of her time in a drunken haze. I knew my father, but I would only see him every so often. He was in a relationship with another woman and was consumed by that household. The only other immediate family I had was my sister who was nine years older than me, but she had a life of her own with her own challenges.

I looked forward to high school. I expected it to be better than my traumatic middle school experience. I can definitely say it was drastically different. I was fourteen and a freshman in high school. Let me give you the full picture. I was a naïve, sheltered, and inexperienced fourteen-year-old freshman. My life consisted of me going to and from school, doing my homework, skating, and/or riding my bike. I existed in my own little world unaware of the dangers that lurked in the shadows of my life.

One day, a car drove next to me while I was skating. The man in the car talked to me. He looked like a teenager, but he was older, especially since he was driving. I am not sure if it showed on my face, but I was shocked and surprised that he, let alone anyone, talked to me outside of my family and a handful of friends, of course. I was especially surprised by him because he had a car! Imagine that! He had stopped to talk to me! I was experiencing feelings I'd never felt before. It was exhilarating and enticing. Did I mention he was cute? Well, he was! His name was Charles. He had a friend who lived in my neighborhood, and he noticed me when I was riding my bike in the area.

After a few conversations during chance meetings, or so I thought, I gave Charles my phone number, and we talked more frequently. Charles was eighteen, and an upperclassman at our high school. There was only a four-year difference between us, but to me, he seemed much older than eighteen. I did not quite understand why Charles would ignore me when I saw him at school even though we talked daily outside of school. In my immature mind, I made it ok that he didn't speak to me at school, so long as I could talk to him after school. The more we talked, the more I needed to talk to him. We talked on the phone and met whenever we could. I craved his attention. For the first time someone saw me, and they wanted to talk to me. The attention Charles gave me was what my soul hungered for. I ate up everything he said. He wouldn't talk about anything significant, but I was happy simply because he was talking to me!

Excited does not describe the feelings I experienced when Charles asked me to go out with him. I couldn't wait until we would spend time together, just the two of us. Of course, he didn't come to my house to pick me up. I would ride my bike to his friend's house, and we would leave from there. The attention I received from Charles had my head and heart reeling. I believed that I was in love with him. I was hooked, and willing to do whatever I needed to do to keep him interested in and spending alone time with me. It wasn't long before Charles and I had sex. Yep, I lost my virginity to Charles at the immature age of fourteen. What I didn't know then was that I was being groomed.

My first time wasn't what I expected at all. I did not experience any of the romantic, wistful escapades that teenage girls daydreamed about. It wasn't like the sensual sex scenes on television, either. If I am being honest, it hurt. He was not concerned about it being my first time only his satisfaction. It left me feeling extremely uncomfortable, tainted and dirty. My first sexual experience was horrible!

Charles did not feel the same way about the experience. It became the only thing we did when we would 'go out.' What I did not realize is that it was the only reason he kept coming around. And, because I craved the attention, I continued to meet with him to have sex. I started feeling guilty about what we were doing. I was sneaking around and having sex, even though I knew it wasn't right. But this is what the popular girls did, right? I wanted so badly to fit in with the 'in crowd.'

I had this down to a science. I could sneak in and out of the house without my mom noticing. Her alcoholism made her unaware of my comings and goings. Most nights she was either drunk or asleep. I used her inattention as an excuse to continue spending time with Charles. That is until I got caught. I remember one time when my mom caught me coming in late. Instead of her lecturing me on the birds and the bees, she took me to the clinic. I guess in her mind, putting me on birth control pills was the solution.

After I lost my virginity to Charles, I became even more attached to him. I was in love. I was hooked. I wanted to spend every waking moment with him and shout to the world that we were in love. At school, I looked for Charles. I would intentionally be where I knew he would be. I would pass by his locker when he would be there, talking with his friends. Nothing seemed to work. Not even when I walked by him in the cafeteria. Charles continued to ignore me at school.

I desperately wanted him to talk to me in public, to ask me to be his girlfriend and to tell his friends about me. I just could not understand how he would only talk to me outside of school, and have sex with me, but ignore me any other time. I didn't think I wanted too much. Did I?

The cycle continued. Charles ignored me repeatedly at school. I would still answer his phone calls and meet him to have sex. Whatever he wanted me to do, I did, just to spend time with him. I would have done anything to keep his attention. I was hooked. I was thirsty for the smallest morsel of attention from Charles. Even when he disrespected me, I would still come back for more. It was all about Charles and what he wanted. I was being used in a one-sided relationship and did not realize it.

There wasn't any consideration for my feelings or my desires. Time after time, Charles would come up with some of the most disgusting sexual encounters. There was this one time when Charles decided he wanted to have sex outside. That night, I allowed Charles to convince me to have sex with him behind the convenience store at the end of my street. It was worse than I could have ever imagined. It was extremely dark, stinky, and trashy behind the store. After our encounter, I realized why it was so smelly behind the building. Apparently, there was dog poop on the ground, and I had been lying in it! I was beyond disgusted! However, that did not take the cake. When I told Charles that I had been lying in poop, he laughed! I was disgusted, devastated, and embarrassed, and all he could do was laugh. I thought he would be sincere and apologetic, but all I got was gut-busting laughter. I couldn't believe it!

My regrets over this situation went far beyond the poop issue. I couldn't believe that I had agreed to have sex on the ground and behind a convenience store. I was disgusted with him, myself, and the whole situation. Not only did Charles convince me to have sex in one of the most disgusting places imaginable, he even convinced me to have sex at one of the most holy places. On several occasions, Charles and I would go to a church parking lot to have sex. Each time, I regretted doing it. This was an all-time low for me.

This back and forth, lowdown, dirty relationship with Charles continued for a couple of years. I continued to have sex with him, and I yearned for him to validate me as his girlfriend. Then came the straw that broke the camel's back. I had been feeling uncomfortable in my vaginal area for at least 2 to 3 months. The discomfort worsened, so I had to tell my mother about it. She didn't ask any questions. I didn't even get a lecture on safe sex. She just took me to the clinic.

At the clinic, they did several tests and determined that I had contracted a sexually transmitted disease (STD). I was devastated. Charles had given me an STD! Thankfully, it was curable. I just couldn't get over the fact that Charles had given me an STD. That was it. I was done!

The next day, I met with Charles. I told him I had gone to the clinic, and I had an STD. Charles asked, "Where did you get it from?" I felt disgusted all over again. I had not been with anyone other than Charles, so there was no doubt that the disease came from him. Charles had the nerve to accuse me of sleeping around. I was so mad at him I could have hit him.

This was the guy to whom I had lost my virginity. I thought about all the filthy situations that I had put myself in to please him. Now, he was accusing me of being a whore! I couldn't believe it! I couldn't take it anymore. Charles had used and disrespected me one too many times. Believing I needed to do whatever it took to keep him had me holding onto this toxic relationship. I believed if I let him go, no one else would want me. I was afraid of going back to feeling useless, alone, and incomplete.

One thing I knew for sure was that I could no longer be with him. I decided this was the last time he was going to cause me pain. I had allowed Charles to degrade me for far too long. He didn't have any respect for himself or me. As we sat in front of his friend's house, I told him I couldn't do this anymore. I told him I no longer wanted to be in a relationship with him. Then I got out of his car and walked home alone, dejected, hurt, shameful and disgusted at myself more than him for allowing this to go on this long.

A Deeper Look…

Here I am, a fourteen-year-old child, taking part in adult activities. I was confused, hurt, and feeling as if the pain I was experiencing from breaking things off with Charles was the same as my constant companion during middle school. How can two different situations cause the same type of pain? I realize now it was because I hated myself as much in middle school as I did in high school. I gave a piece of myself, my self-esteem, and my self-respect away in both instances to boys who weren't worthy of even tying my shoes.

Why did I do that to myself? Because no one ever paid attention to me, so I was starving for attention. I didn't differentiate between bad attention or good attention. In both instances, it was attention, and it was more than what I was getting at home and from those who were supposed to love me! I had been overlooked and unnoticed for years, and out of nowhere this cute boy wanted to talk to me. I believed he saw me, really saw me, and was interested in getting to know me for who I am. It never occurred to me he was just using me to get what he wanted from me. It was emotionally overwhelming for an attention-starved teenage girl.

In hindsight, I see Charles was a predator in search of his prey. He had a motive, and he sensed the vulnerabilities in me. He led me on with the promise of a boyfriend-girlfriend relationship. I was so caught up in the idea of having a boyfriend; I didn't notice the signs. Even in my misery, I justified our age difference because we attended the same school. Earlier I stated I was addicted to him. I understand now that I was not addicted to him, but I latched onto him because I craved the attention that he offered when no one else in my life was giving me any. I was in way over my head!

It wasn't long before I realized Charles was very cunning. Charles had me beat on so many levels, including maturity. I could tell Charles had been around the block a few times. He wasn't new to "the game," and he took advantage of my naivety. What I experienced in middle school, prepared me to become the victim in my story with Charles. When I ended that relationship, it was me taking back my power and learning how to put me first. I have been told the quickest way to get anywhere is to take the first step. I am so proud of myself today for taking that first step.

There are so many things I wish were different while growing up. I finally realize they all contributed to me being who I am today and to me telling my story. No fourteen-year-old-girl needs to be put in that position, but it happens in homes throughout the world every day. A regret I think I will always have is not doing things God's way and waiting until marriage, to give my husband the gift of my virginity.

I also wish my mom had paid closer attention. Perhaps, she would have picked up on the signs that I was changing. I believe she would have been able to tell I was going astray had she not been in a drunken state most of the time. I don't blame her for my decisions. I just wish that she could have provided more guidance for me as a teen.

One of the greatest lessons of my life is when I learned having sex with someone doesn't always lead to or represent a relationship or love. Something that didn't become apparent, if I am being honest until after I engaged in several more lifeless relationships. Why did it take me so long? Because I had a negative self-image and self-esteem. I did not see my own beauty and when others realized that was my reality, they decided I was a safe place to land for a while. It took me years to face who I am, how I see me, what I was doing to myself and how I felt about the woman looking back at me in the mirror.

It wasn't until many years later that I understood soul ties and how they affected my life and my future relationships. I had opened myself up to sensations and feelings that my body craved even though I knew it wasn't something I needed to or sometimes wanted to take part in. I fought with those feelings daily. They didn't go away overnight.

I wish I could say I never saw Charles again, and after the breakup, I turned my life around. Unfortunately, that's not the case. That soul tie was strong! A few years after our relationship ended, Charles found me and attempted to start a "new" relationship with me. Even after the horrific relationship that we had, something within me thought it would be okay to try again. I know crazy, right?!

I invited Charles into my home. Can you guess what he wanted? You guessed it. It was still all about sex. Absolutely nothing had changed about him since I saw him last. Charles hadn't matured at all. I was still dealing with eighteen-year-old Charles. What was I thinking? I couldn't have been thinking! My place of hurt was yearning for something to focus on other than the pain that was my constant companion. I needed to be healed and sleeping with Charles again was not going to get me the healing I needed. I felt unworthy of a loving relationship and found myself constantly settling for the unhealthy ones because they were familiar.

Something within me knew I couldn't allow him back into my life. I thank God daily I had the strength to say no. This time I chose myself regardless of what my body wanted or craved for. I had to stop the emotional and mental bleeding. I needed to begin my journey to healing. Like the woman with the issue of blood, somehow, I knew if I could just get to Jesus. If I could just touch the hem of His garment, I would be made whole. The question before me was how was I going to get to Him and am I strong enough to do what it would take for me to be healed? I don't know where the strength came from to tell him no! Today I can declare and decree that it was all God!

It would have been tragic for me to allow him back into my life. I can't even begin to fathom what that would have done to me emotionally, physically, and spiritually. What would that have done to that drop of self-esteem that I had discovered within me at the time? Thank you, God, for covering me and keeping me in that moment, even when I didn't really want to be kept!

After my relationship with Charles, I had other relationships. I was still looking for love in all the wrong places. I had witnessed my mother deal with deadbeats, and I learned how to attract them and keep them in my life without really owning up to the fact that they were only taking up space. They were incapable of giving me what I needed. I was in a battle that only God could equip me to handle. I want to stop here and say something. Generational curses are real! My mother dealt with deadbeats, my sister dealt with deadbeats, and I dealt with deadbeats.

It was like being stuck in a never-ending cycle of bad relationships. I always tried to make them work. I wanted to see the best in everyone because I didn't want anyone to leave me. I felt as if I had to hold onto everyone who came into my life. I moved from one relationship to the next, picking up more and more soul ties along the way. The cycle, the deeply rooted generational curse, had to be broken, and I was determined to become the curse breaker!

It took developing a personal relationship with God to break the generational curse that had attached itself to me! As I am thinking about this, I am reminded of Matthew 17:21 (HCSB) that says, "*…this kind does not come out except by prayer and fasting.*" Once I began my healing journey with God there was a lot of both going on. Because I was determined not to return to who I was. I wanted everything that God had for me and said in His word I could have.

I attempted to make excuses about the revolving door of men in my life. No, not everyone was a deadbeat, but if I wanted something different, I had to do something different. With that being said, I had to recognize my attraction to every man I had dated up to and during that time was because they had deadbeat ways, and that was a safe place for me. God showed me I didn't need a man to feel complete. All I needed was Him! I needed to let His love teach me how to love the woman looking back at me in the mirror and be what completed me. God reminded me in Colossians 2:10 (NASB), "*…in Him you have been made complete, and He is the head over all rule and authority…*

I had made a mess of my life far before I valued myself, my life, or the destiny that God had for me. I thought I had gone too far to ever come back, but that wasn't how my story ends. God is giving me the pen to re-write the ending of my story every day!

I see now that even then, God had His ever-loving hands on me, and they were wrapped tightly around me. God had a plan for me. Jeremiah 29:11 (NIV) always speaks to my soul. It says, "*For I know the plans I have for you, declares the Lord, plans to prosper you and not to harm you, plans to give you hope and a future.*" He spoke His plan into and over my life, long before my existence. Before I could accept the plan, He has for my life and the purpose for my birth, I had to listen to, take in, and understand what God said to Jeremiah in Jeremiah 1:5, *"Before I formed you in the womb I knew you, and before you were born I consecrated you; I appointed you…"*

Are you wondering how I realized I needed to have a personal relationship with Jesus Christ? My mom and I didn't attend a church regularly. However, as a child, I occasionally attended church with family members and close friends. It was then that the seeds were being planted in my life that I am reaping the harvest from today.

By my late teens and early twenties, I had grown to know and love the Lord. The closer I got to God, the more my past weighed heavily on me. I did not fully understand the gift of self-forgiveness, and I condemned myself for the horrible things I had done in my life. I questioned myself and my worthiness. How in the world could I have done this? How could I stoop so low as to have sex on church grounds?

I was broken. The enemy convinced me that I was not worthy of a better life and future. He knew something I did not know. Although I knew God had forgiven me, I hadn't forgiven myself. As long as I carried that guilt around, I was not fully walking in my healing. God took me on a journey to help me forgive myself. He intentionally navigated my life where I finally realized and accepted all aspects of my healing and not just the parts that weren't as dirty.

I am a firm believer that nothing happens by coincidence. Everything that happens in our lives, whether good or bad, has purpose. During moments of insecurity, I would ask myself: 'How in the world could becoming sexually active at fourteen be purposeful in my life?' Genesis 50:20 (HCSB) says it best. It says *"…You planned evil against me; God planned it for good to bring about the present result—the survival of many people."* God planned for me to share my testimony with you to encourage you to choose a better path.

God healed me from the hurt and condemnation I inflicted on myself in a moment in time that is forever seared into my heart and mind. I was a member of a small but powerful book club. We were discussing a chapter in a book about the "F" word, FORGIVENESS! I remember thinking,

"God, who do I need to forgive?" I was so focused on trying to figure out who I needed to forgive outside of myself when God told me to forgive myself. Forgive myself? For what? I certainly had a long laundry list of things that had happened in my life. God revealed He wanted me to forgive myself for having sex at fourteen and for having sex in the church parking lot.

My journey to healing took me down paths I never thought I would travel. One of those paths led to me forgiving myself. It was hard! I had been harboring ill feelings towards myself for more years than I can remember. God knew I needed to be set free from the hatred I had towards myself because of my past. He led me to go sit in the same church parking lot where I had sex with Charles on more than one occasion. God told me to journal my thoughts and feelings word for word. He told me to write as if I was fourteen-year-old Pam again.

I sat there, in that church's parking lot, writing out my feelings and everything related to becoming sexually active at fourteen. He then told me to journal about how nasty I felt, my sadness, and the anger I harbored towards myself for allowing myself to be treated that way. I can't tell you how long I was in that church parking lot. I do know I stayed until every ounce of shame, sadness, nastiness, anger, disgust, and hurt was written on the pages of that journal. I journaled until the words stopped flowing. The last tear I would ever shed over my past is memorialized on the pages of that journal.

As the tears flowed and the words filled each page of my journal, the freer I became. The tears washed away the vestiges of my past from my heart and mind! In that parking lot, God healed me. I was free from what I previously allowed to define me. I accepted those actions were merely a page in the story of my life. What is so powerful about the entire moment is God took me to the same place that led to my hurt, so He could heal my hurt! Did you catch that in your spirit?

God doesn't do the expected. He does the unexpected to bring about change. God returned me to my place of pain, shame, and hatred to heal me, all while replacing those feelings with His love. Don't run away from the place where your hurt began. Give God the opportunity to take you back to that place! Allow Him to reveal His power! Open your heart so God can show you that everything you went through was necessary. He wants to show you how He will bring goodness out of every painful, shameful, evil, and/or hated thing in your life. He desires to heal your hurt and restore you to the place of honor He has awaiting you! In my life, He is a healer!!! He is the mender of broken pieces. He has proven time and time again that He is the only one who can put your broken pieces back together perfectly!

I didn't realize how broken I was at fourteen. I didn't realize it was just the beginning of what would become a continuous journey of my brokenness. Pieces of me were scattered amongst the boys and men I slept with over the years. God reminded me in Psalm 51:17 (NIV) that no matter what I had done, He will never despise me. His word says, *"My sacrifice, O God, is a broken spirit; a broken and contrite heart you, God will not despise."* I implore you to take your broken pieces to Him! It will be the best decision of your life.

My acts weren't justified. Sin is sin, but I knew I had to stop condemning myself. For me condemnation was much harder because it was self-inflicted. Conviction is from God, and it's done out of His love for us to help us live righteously. Romans 8:1 (NKJV) helped paint a clear picture for me. *"There is therefore no condemnation to those who are in Christ Jesus, who do not walk according to the flesh, but according to the Spirit."*

Charles had to be a piece of my puzzle. I had to walk the path I walked to be the phenomenal woman I am today. My path was hand carved by our Almighty God. As I mentioned earlier, He is working it all out for my good! I better understand how my broken pieces have helped me to grow. Those experiences orchestrated my move into my God-given destiny! Romans 8:28 (NIV), *"And we know that in all things God works for the good of those who love Him, who have been called according to His purpose."*

God is a healer of the broken-hearted, the ignored, the abused, and the abuser. He is able to heal us from whatever we've been through and whatever we're going through! He can heal us from the self-inflicted pain of condemnation and the pain we've inflicted upon others.

Through God's grace, I have learned to embrace my past. I know that part of my story makes me who I am today. I am learning more about Him every day. Our personal relationship is growing and becoming even more intimate. His unconditional love has helped me to grow, know, and love myself. The more I learned about how He has forgiven me of all my sins, the more I could forgive myself. In Ephesians 1:7 (NKJV) I learned, "*...in Him we have redemption through His blood, the forgiveness of sins, according to the riches of His grace!*" Micah 7:19 says, "*He will turn again, he will have compassion upon us; he will subdue our iniquities; and thou wilt cast all their sins into the depths of the sea.*" I came to understand myself better, and I could see my past in a better light.

Thank you, Jesus, for making all things new in my life. He has turned my mess into the message you are reading now. That's the God I serve. Thank you, God, for saving a wretch like me!

There are days when I have to remind myself of this truth. Sometimes my pieces become scattered, and I have to ask God to come in and do His perfect work. That is when the beautifully broken pieces fit together to show me the beautiful mosaic of who God created me to be. I am reminded of Psalms 147:3 (NIV) "*He heals the brokenhearted and binds up their wounds.*" Each of us is "**Beautifully Broken**," and God is our mender!

I was the little chocolate chic, the shy girl who allowed her poor decisions to define her. Now, I'm walking in the daily strength that God gives me. I not only live and walk in my truth, but I help other women do the same. This is my truth. This is my story, and I am finally embracing and owning it. Freedom feels good! I'm no longer bound. God has removed my shackles. Thank You, God! I am free!

God built me to be an overcomer! "*And they overcame him by the blood of the Lamb and by the word of their testimony, and they did not love their lives to their death*". Revelations 12:11 (NKJV). Despite how it happened, it happened for a reason. I am still here to tell my story and help others tell theirs.

We all have a story to tell. Don't be quiet! Don't be shy! Don't run away from your truth! Share your story with the world. Be an inspiration to yourself and so many others. Someone is waiting for you to share your truth. They need what you have. They need to hear my story and yours. I am Built to Overcome! And you, too, are Built to Overcome!

Love Covers

One day, I went to the local electronics store. I was in the store browsing around. Eventually, I found my way to the music department and started looking for a CD. I was in the store for about ten minutes when suddenly I heard a voice say, "Do you need some help?"

I looked up, and there stood this tall, dark, and handsome guy. He was looking at me with a slight smile on his face. Although I was feeling his good looks, my response was, "Do you work here?"

He said, "No, but I can help you find a CD."

My sarcastic response was, "So you're just walking through the store helping people, but you don't work here?"

His comeback was, "You look like you needed some help." I'm sure that I had a slightly sarcastic look mixed with a grin. Then it hit me. He was flirting with me! He decided to help me find a CD as an excuse to talk to me.

I entertained his small talk for a few more minutes and allowed him to help me find a CD. After everything was said and done, he asked for my number. I told him I don't give my number to strange men because he could be a stalker. We both laughed, but I was so serious. I told him he could give me his number, and he did.

When he gave me his number, it came with instructions. I was told to call on a certain day and at a certain time. Apparently, that's the time that he would be at his aunt's house. I remember thinking, "Why doesn't this grown man have his own phone?" After that, I didn't think about it anymore.

I was in such a hurry to talk to him. There I go again, acting thirsty. Slow down, take a deep breath, and get your bearings. Don't make it so evident you are tired of being single. Anticipation got the best of me because I was SO ready for a new relationship that I called him the day before he told me to call. The lady who answered the phone was really nice. She said she would tell him I called when he got there. The next day, my phone rang, and it was him calling me back.

We talked over the phone. What seemed to be so great about him was his honesty. I didn't have to drag any information out of him. He told me everything. Although most of his story wasn't great, I found out a lot of things about him and his past within a very short period of time.

We talked several times throughout the days prior to our next meeting. I found out he had been married and divorced. He supposedly had two daughters (who may or may not be his since he and his wife were both entertaining other relationships during their marriage). I was told he lost his mother at a very early age, and the struggles he had been through after she passed away were horrific. Most shockingly, I had met him on Monday, and he had just gotten out of prison on the previous Friday. Oh, my goodness, what in the world did I just walk into?

Considering all this, I willingly walked into this relationship. My eyes were wide open. He hadn't withheld any information from me and any questions I asked, he answered. Most of what I heard was enough for me to run as fast as I could in the opposite direction. But there was an attraction there, or so I thought. Within the first couple of weeks, God had shown me many reasons to not continue in this relationship, yet I continued!

One of our very first dates was at a popular seafood restaurant. I remember being so mad at him because he only wanted to eat the cheddar biscuits. "I know the bread is delicious, but please order more than that,"

I thought. Later, I realized why he only wanted bread. Terrell didn't come from much and didn't have much, as he was recently released from prison. I guess I can say he was being a gentleman by not ordering food for which I would have to pay. But it didn't take long for him to become comfortable with me paying for things.

Our first restaurant date was just the beginning of our story. From there, we became a couple. Terrell eventually found a job and was eager to move from his town to mine. I was eager for him to move because his town wasn't a short drive at all. After he started working, and we were well into our relationship, I agreed to get an apartment in my name for him. We had been talking about getting married. I thought once we were married, I could just move into the apartment with him and live happily ever after.

Things were moving quickly between us. I allowed things to move much faster than they should have. God's voice began softly. Eventually, it turned into yelling. My Heavenly Father wanted me to yield, but I was too busy speeding past all the red flags, bright flashing lights, warning signs, and stop lights that were glaringly obvious. God had hit me in the head with a spiritual brick or two, but I was still going full speed ahead in the wrong direction. I can't say God didn't give me signs to slow down or cause me to end the relationship.

I remember sitting in my Pastor's office and telling him about Terrell. I mentioned I had prayed, and God had given me just what I asked for- tall, dark, and handsome. My Pastor laughed boisterously that day. He has one of those contagious laughs, but this one was even funnier. We both laughed. After he finished laughing, he said, "Oh, is that right?" I said, "Yes, sir. He is everything I need."

Pastor and Terrell developed a wonderful relationship. They would talk outside of church and meet for breakfast. Terrell eventually became his armor bearer and was being groomed to become a deacon in training. Terrell seemed to have so many noble qualities. On the outside, he looked like a well-oiled machine, especially at church.

Terrell and I had some good times during our relationship. I remember he made our first Valentine's Day special. Terrell hadn't saved enough money to buy a car, so he took a cab to my workplace and hand-delivered my gifts. I received an email from security informing me that someone was in the lobby waiting for me. When I got to the lobby, I saw it was Terrell with roses and a charm bracelet. I was so excited, and I felt all bubbly inside. When it comes to love and matters of the heart, I am beyond emotional on holidays. I overlooked the part that he had arrived in a cab. "Why didn't he just have them delivered?" I thought. Anyway, the gifts were beautiful.

We had been dating about four months. We were already talking about marriage, and we looked at rings several times. I knew Terrell's finances were tight as he rebuilt his life, and money for a ring was not in the cards right then. The more we talked about getting married, the more excited I became. I opened an account at one of the jewelry stores and we decided to get our wedding rings on credit. Terrell assured me he would make the monthly payments. This was yet another sign and a big mistake on my part. God's voice was becoming increasingly louder and louder. It had changed from a whisper to a very audible voice. God was yelling trying to get my attention, but I wasn't listening.

There is absolutely no reason I should have opened that account, expecting him to make the payments. I was hoping and wishing on a wing and a prayer. I hoped he would pay because he was working. However, that wasn't a guarantee.

In years past, my mom had told me to not get so many credit cards, but I didn't listen to her either. By the time I was a young adult, I had ruined my credit. I worked like crazy to fix it, and I was extremely proud of myself for getting it done. Now, my A-1 credit was at risk of possibly being destroyed again. All because of a man and because I would not listen to God telling me to slow down and heed His warnings.

I was working for a very profitable Fortune 500 company that paid very well. Terrell didn't have a phone. I wanted to easy access to him, so I added another phone to my existing cell phone account for him. I was still living at home with my mom, so I could afford it, even if he didn't pay his portion. I was already becoming comfortable paying for everything concerning Terrell, which was a huge mistake!

Terrell knew exactly how many minutes and text messages allowed per month with "our" cell phone plan. He knew we had to share the allowable minutes and text messages. When the first bill came, it was more than $800. I thought there was no way that could be right. There had to be some sort of mistake. I called customer service to inquire about the bill. As the representative explained the usage, I could feel my blood pressure rising. I could feel myself getting hotter. My temperature was literally rising. If I could have checked my blood pressure at that moment, I'm sure that it would have been through the roof!

The usage on Terrell's line alone was far more than our shared plan allowed. I was out of control mad. I couldn't believe that he would do that to me. Not only did he go over our call minutes, but the text messages had tripled. Our texts to one another were unlimited because we had the same carrier and the same shared plan. Who was he texting so much to cause this more than $800 bill? I looked at the bill and kept seeing the same unfamiliar number repeatedly. I pulled some strings and found out who the number belonged to. It was a female's number, and not just any female, but a female I knew. She attended our church! My blood pressure was now past the sky and into the clouds.

I was suspicious of his interactions with this young lady for a while. I had asked him about their conversations before. It seemed like they were talking a lot at church. I confronted Terrell about the phone bill. We argued. I asked him what they had to talk about so much and so often. His response was unbelievable. He told me he was helping her with the problems she was having with her boyfriend. Excuse me?!? You're willing to lose your girlfriend and soon-to-be wife because you want to help another woman with her boyfriend issues?!? Wow! I couldn't believe it. The plot was thickening, and the screams from God turned to silence. I felt God had taken His hands off the situation.

Terrell was working, but he wasn't making a lot of money. He definitely wasn't making enough to pay his portion of the phone bill. As I sat thinking about everything, I came to the realization that I had a few options available to me:

Option 1: I could walk away from the relationship.

Option 2: I could find this woman and confront her. I knew this wouldn't be lady-like or Christian-like, but that's how mad I was over the situation.

Option 3: I could realize that people make mistakes and try to fix what was broken in our relationship.

Terrell knew I was beyond mad about the entire situation. If he loved me and wanted to marry me, there was no reason he should have been texting another woman. I didn't know how to feel. I didn't know if I wanted to fix it. I didn't know if I wanted to yell, scream, curse, fight, cry, or all the above. I honestly didn't know what to do.

There I go again, being the chick who always sees the good in everyone while wearing blinders to what's right in front of my face. As a wise person once told me, "When people show you who they are, believe them!" It was time for me to listen to something other than my heart and hormones. I willingly entered this relationship thinking Terrell was who I needed and wanted, the man God had given me to share my life and love with. It became abundantly clear to me I couldn't continuously deal with situations like this. What's a girl to do?

Terrell had studied me in the short time we'd known each other. He knew me inside and out. He had listened to the things I shared with him about my past, especially my past relationships. This allowed him to manipulate me. He knew exactly what to say and do in that moment to take the pain away. The situation called for a cooling-off period, and I didn't see Terrell for a few days after our big argument. A few days later, he asked me to come to his apartment. I agreed to stop by, but I told him I wouldn't come inside. I was still upset about the bill, and I still wasn't over what happened.

When Terrell walked outside, he sat in the car with me. Then we both got out of the car and continued to talk in the parking lot. As we were talking, he leaned in close to me, reached into his pocket, and pulled out an engagement ring. It was the same ring I had opened the credit card account to purchase. I was shocked! I couldn't believe this was THE moment. Terrell was actually going to propose to me! He took the ring out and placed it on my finger. He told me he loved me and gave me a hug. I thought, "Is this really how he's going to propose to me?" I mean, we were in the parking lot of an apartment complex.

Terrell explained he wanted to spend the rest of his life with me. And right there in the parking lot, he asked me to marry him. Despite my doubts and all the warning signs, I said yes. As you can imagine, I got caught up in the moment. This was my very own fairytale proposal. Of course, it wasn't as I had imagined. But I couldn't say no, right? I was really going to be married. I was going to be someone's wife!

Deep down I knew I deserved more, but I settled for what was in my face for the present. I felt like this could all be great, and this could all be hell at the same time. I didn't know what was to come. All I knew was I wanted to be married, and I loved him.

I told a coworker that I was getting married. "What's the rush?" he asked. Why hadn't I stopped to consider this? "There's no rush. We're both ready to be married," I replied. The truth is, we were only about six months into our relationship. It was definitely a quick engagement.

It was obvious my sister had her own opinion about the whole situation. She made it known she didn't care for Terrell. She told me he wasn't ready for marriage because he wasn't stable enough. Deep down, I knew my sister only wanted the best for me. I knew what she was saying was all out of love. She was older and wiser. She knew I deserved more. I believed I couldn't simply walk away.

One day, we were eating at one of our favorite restaurants. Terrell, my sister, and my mom were all there. We were talking about our wedding plans and deciding who was going to be in the wedding. That's when my sister said she wouldn't be in my wedding. She said it so adamantly and with the coldest look on her face. I was crushed! I started crying. I mean, it was one of those heartbreaking, soul-stirring outbursts.

My sister can definitely be stubborn. When her mind is made up, it's made up- nothing left to discuss! My tears and sobbing didn't move her one bit! Her answer was NO! Sadly, I had to accept it because she wasn't budging. At that moment, it felt like she was the most heartless person in the world. I knew she was just being protective. I told myself it was all out of love. My sister had spoken, period. She said she would come to the wedding, but she wouldn't be in the wedding.

Even after those big signs from God, I still proceeded with the wedding. I said yes to the dress and to Terrell! We would have a small wedding party. I had two friends who would be my maid of honor and matron of honor. He had two best men.

Somehow, I pulled together a wedding. Our budget was minimal, but we still had a wedding venue, photographer, and catering- just the necessities. We got married at our church. My gown was absolutely beautiful, and it was a really nice ceremony. I smiled a lot and enjoyed my day. Underneath my smile, was a feeling of doubt. I wondered if this day should really happen! Was I making the right decision?

Our reception was at the community center, close to our church. Everything seemed to turn out so nicely. Having my closest family and friends there made the day extra special for me. Some co-workers also attended, and I met some of Terrell's family for the very first time.

We had jumped the broom! We had tied the knot! The wedding was a success. It was modest, but lovely. Terrell and I had a nice weekend honeymoon. That was all we could afford. It seemed like the perfect little getaway. It was a glimpse of happiness.

I was now Mrs. Terrell Jones. But what did that mean? Would Terrell fulfill the vows he made to me before God on our wedding day? Would he love and cherish me, for better or worse, 'til death do us part? Would he honor me as his wife, as a man should? I was no longer under my daddy's covering. My last name had changed, and now Terrell was responsible for my well-being. Would he look out for me and keep my best interest at heart? Would he make sure I had everything I needed when I needed it? Only time would tell.

The beautiful apartment I got for Terrell before we were married would become our first home together. It was a nice, cozy apartment on the east side of town. Unfortunately, we wouldn't be able to stay there long.

The job Terrell had before we were married didn't last long after the wedding. The rent for our apartment, along with the other bills, became my burden alone. I was coming home from long days at work to eviction notices on my door! Wait a minute! I was raised by a single mother who made less than minimum wage, and I don't ever recall seeing an eviction notice on our door. How did I go from the life that I was living with my mom to something worse after marriage?

We were less than three months into our marriage, and I was already feeling like it was going downhill. This wasn't looking good at all. I had a big balance due on our lovely apartment. I couldn't afford to pay it in addition to all our other bills, so I had to look for a less expensive apartment. What did that mean? It meant that I was likely going back to an area I didn't prefer. This was the life I chose. I had to make the best of it.

I found an apartment close to my mom. It was in a supposedly better area, not too deep in the hood. It was not what I wanted, though. I wasn't excited about it, but it was going to be our home for a while. Thank God that it was just the two of us, because our new place was extremely small. Seriously, it was so small that we could barely turn around without bumping into something. There wasn't even an official parking lot, so we had to park just outside of our front door in a makeshift parking space. It wasn't great, but at that moment, it was all I could afford.

Although I tried to find peace with my circumstances, I couldn't stand that apartment. It was horrible! Were things worse because I was married to Terrell? How did I go from better to worse? Shouldn't it have gone the other way around?

Somehow, I survived until I could get caught up on the bills and save enough money to get out of there. God was still taking care of us. I was so grateful when the lease on that tiny apartment expired. I was able to find another nice apartment complex on the east side of town again. It was a well-kept hidden gem, and I was so thankful that God allowed me to find them. The apartments were tucked off the road and under a canopy of trees. I felt like I had arrived. It was cozy and decent. There were nice amenities, including a picnic area and a pond with a fountain in it. I was moving back up again. There would be no more hood-living for me. Thank you, God!

As with most marriages, hard times will arise. Eventually, we hit another snag in the road. The finances became tight again. The rent was late again. We were about to be put out of another apartment. What could I do? Who could I ask for help?

I asked our church for financial support. I was over the finance committee at our church, so it was heartbreaking and embarrassing to have to ask our church family for money. When there was a financial need by a church member, it had to be approved by our Pastor first. Then he would give the okay for the finance committee to cut the check. I was aware of the process. My heart hurt, and my pride took a hit when I had to ask the church for help. The finance committee members issued the check after getting our Pastor's approval. We received the assistance we needed to help us with our rent. Thank you, God! To my chagrin that wasn't the end of the whole ordeal.

We were a small church. Everybody knew everybody. However, financial matters should always remain confidential, right? Unfortunately, there was a leak in our "old building", or more accurately, there was a leak in somebody's mouth.

The news was out that we had to get money from the church. The gossip was spreading. Everyone at church knew about our financial struggle.

When the news got back to me, my feelings were so hurt. I was crushed. The people I worshipped with, laughed with, and went out with outside of church were talking about me behind my back. Then they were laughing and talking with me as if they hadn't done a thing. I couldn't believe it!

Although it was gossip, it was the truth. We had to borrow money from the church, but it shouldn't have become a matter of discussion throughout the church. Why did it spread from the finance committee room to members of the congregation? That hurt the most. We had confided in our church leaders. Now, everyone knew our business, and it didn't have to be that way. It wasn't supposed to be that way.

When I needed their prayers and desired to feel their loving embrace, I got slapped in the face by their laughter. It was painful. But I prayed and prayed some more about the situation. I wanted to forgive. I didn't want to hold a grudge against the people who talked about me behind my back. It took some time. Eventually, I let it go. Although, I never forgot about it.

For me, these times were especially hard pills to swallow. I knew if Terrell would keep a job, things would be better for us. I hoped he would, but it didn't happen. We continued to struggle financially. My fairytale was becoming a nightmare. Lord, why didn't I say, "I Don't!?"

A Deeper Look…

I walked into that electronics store not knowing that I was walking into the next chapter of my life. What was supposed to be a moment turned into what would eventually seem like a never-ending story. It became a very long, uncomfortable, and painful chapter of my life that began with a brief encounter.

Terrell was everything I thought I wanted. He was tall, dark, and handsome. Those were the specifics I had asked of God. How foolish of me! Did I really think that tall, dark, and handsome were the only requirements for the keys to my heart? Unfortunately, that's where I was in life. In my mind, the only thing that mattered was the outside appearance. Talk about being wrong!

I felt like "he's the one" because he was handsome, and he showed an interest in me. I jumped in before taking the time to get to know Terrell. Before I knew it, I was already head-over-hills in love. But who is he really? I didn't take the time to dig deeper and get to know him. I was still in the superficial stage of the relationship when everything seemed just peachy. I had focused more on his outer covering, instead of getting to know who he really was and what was in his heart. This was teaching me a valuable lesson. I needed to learn how to go deeper when connecting and attaching myself to someone.

I jumped into the relationship with both feet. I did not heed the warnings or listen when God was speaking. Does anything sound familiar? I was right back to living as if I did not have a personal relationship with God, as if His opinion and advice did not matter. I was going to do this thing my way. What a mess! That way of thinking cost me more than I was willing to pay and took more than I was willing to give. Hopefully, I finally understood what God, my co-worker, and my big sister were trying to tell me. Take your time, get to know the other person, and consult God about the matters of the heart. He will never lead me astray. Let me say this because I don't want anyone to get caught up. Stop, think, and WAIT before sharing your heart and giving your body sexually with that special someone or anyone for that matter. Soul ties are real.

I was learning the lesson the hard way! No one can offer me self-worth. My self-worth isn't for sale. It is directly tied to the love God has for me and its healing powers that allows me to see myself the way God sees me. What I didn't realize is that I was trying to find my self-worth in Terrell. I had given him, without realizing it, the responsibility for fixing what was wrong in my life and healing me. It became evident to me very quickly that just beneath the surface, I was still broken! My lack of self-worth and negative self-esteem once again was taking me on a journey of pain, shame, and brokenness that I didn't think I would recover from.

I have always had a big heart. I've always been someone who loves to help people in any way I can. I want for others what seemed to be elusive in my own life. I enjoy helping people feel better about themselves and watching them become better. Falling into the trap many women fall into, I attempted to fix Terrell. As you can imagine, it was colossal failure.

I know I can't fix anyone. More importantly, Terrell wasn't a project or a fixer upper; he was a man and I needed to step back and allow him to be one. My efforts to help him because I loved him and wanted the best for him put me in the position of an enabler. My inability to call him on his mess and challenge him to be better had created the monster who couldn't or wouldn't hold down a job, did not treat me like his most valued possession, and made me a laughingstock at church. There were expectations and boundaries I should have had in place before ever meeting Terrell. If Terrell did not measure up to my expectations or honor my boundaries, I should have been strong enough to walk away.

By not choosing me above everyone else and honoring God first and foremost, I ended up even more broken than before I met him. The small amount of self-esteem I had when I met him was slowly but surely being stripped away. Day by day it was being depleted, leaving me in the negative financially, spiritually, and personally. God instructs men to love their wives as Christ loves the church. He was to be her covering and her protector. Terrell lacked the integrity and the desire to be the covering I needed as my husband and as the spiritual leader in our home. If I am being honest, Terrell's so-called love wasn't even enough to keep me covered on a sunny day. It definitely couldn't keep me dry in a thunderstorm.

Terrell saw nothing wrong with leaving me to manage our finances by myself and struggle to keep a roof over our head while still striving to be a loving wife to him. Where was my strong and loving husband, who was supposed to be my safe place to land? I did not see it; however, I cannot say I did not feel it. Because I did. Maybe my sister could see this long before I did, which is why she refused to be in my wedding. Today, I can clearly see she only wanted the best for me, and she knew Terrell wasn't it.

God operates in our lives under His perfect and permissive will. His permissive will is when we do whatever we want with our life and in most cases, we are not showing God we want His best in our life. The perfect will of God is God's divine plan for our life and is often shown when we understand and give God free reign to manifest Jeremiah 29:11 in our life. Once I stepped outside of God's perfect will, I was functioning fully within His permissive will. If I am being honest, it's not a great place to be in.

Once a Christian accepts Jesus Christ as their Lord and Savior, he/she belongs to Him. God gave the greatest gift ever given just to have a personal relationship with us. He gave us His only begotten Son, and once you make that confession with your mouth and carry its belief in your heart, you belong to Him. God only directs our path when we allow Him to do so. We must make the choice every second of every day to allow His will to be what we follow. Even though we are given the freedom to make our own decisions, there is a cost associated with every choice we make, good or bad.

Keep this in mind, free will isn't always free. Nor does it bode well for you if you don't surrender your free will for God's perfect will to play out in and through your life. As I sit here thinking about Terrell and our marriage, I am ready to admit that God had given me so many warning signs about him. When I failed to adhere and/or heed to His prompting, He took a step back and allowed me to really taste what free will looks, feels, smells, tastes, and sounds like.

Let me take a pause for the cause here and say that even in our mess, Jesus is still talking and giving instructions. It's up to us to listen. Even in our disobedience, He still turns our bad situations into good. He can make all things work together for our good. Romans 8:28 (NKJV) says, *"And we know that all things work together for good to those who love God, to those who are called according to His purpose."*

God wants what's best for us! Be specific in your prayers when you're praying for your husband. Although tall, dark, and handsome is great, consider the more important parts like personality traits, character, religious beliefs, financial responsibility, his upbringing, baby mama drama, etc. Be specific when you talk to God about what you want, need, and desire in your future husband. God does and will grant you the desires of your heart! While you're waiting, prepare yourself to be blessed by drawing closer to God each day. Don't just pray asking God for a husband/mate, learn how to pray for him/her, asking God to give you the insight to be an intercessor praying for their continual spiritual growth and development.

By the time I met Terrell, I was around 23. I knew God. Well, the truth is I knew *of* Him. I had been attending a wonderful church since my late teens. I went to church every Sunday, and I was very active in services, programs, and activities. I was learning more and more about God, but I wasn't really allowing Him to show me where I needed to be mended and healed. I hadn't surrendered my life to Him while relinquishing any and all control I believed I had.

I didn't know when I met Terrell, but he would be the very one who'd drive me to the feet of Jesus! After I re-dedicated my life to Christ, I jokingly told my sister Jesus knew I was going to need Him to make it through my relationship with Terrell. I certainly need Him in every relationship, but my relationship with Terrell was special. Without God, it could have taken me out of here! To be exact, it was approximately one year to the date of marrying Terrell that I got saved. I referred to it as a re-dedication, but I could really say that I got saved and gave my heart to God that night in April 2003.

I know it's said that once saved, always saved. However, before that night, I didn't think I *was* saved. I had been baptized, and I had accepted the right hand of fellowship. I just don't recall ever giving my heart and my life to Christ. I don't think I fully understood what it meant to be saved. There were no doubts or questions in my mind after that night. I knew I was saved wholeheartedly, and I wanted to live for God. I wanted to do my best to live a good, pleasing, and acceptable life for God. I put forth every effort to do so after that fateful night. My relationship with Christ blossomed and grew over the coming years. I would rather do life with God any day than attempt it alone. Trust me when I say I have been there and done that. It isn't worth it. Jesus is the answer for every question in your life.

My relationship with Christ also helped me through that hurtful church situation. I thought I could trust my brothers and sisters at church. I had no idea of the hurt I was about to endure from the people I loved the most, and who were supposed to love me! The gossip mill was in full effect with my financial situation.

Church related issues put a different spin on things. I wasn't ready for this twist! The hurt stung even more. I wasn't ready to realize that "Church Hurt" is a different kind of hurt. Sure, church people are still human beings, just like other people. However, being hurt by my "church family" seemed to make my heart ache a little more. How could they talk about me behind my back? How could they do this to me?

I realized I shouldn't hold a grudge. I wanted to forgive. I didn't want to be mean and nasty to the people that talked about me. I knew I needed to let it go. That was the starting point for a beautiful lesson about healing.

Healing from the wounds inflicted by my fellow church members was hard. It took me a very long time to get over that hurt. Eventually, I was able to forgive, let it go, and move on. Proverbs 4:23 (NKJV) tells us to *"Keep your heart with all diligence, for out of it spring the issues of life."* I wouldn't have been able to attend church services Sunday after Sunday had I not allowed God to purify my heart and take me through the process of forgiveness. The forgiveness was for me, not them. They had gone on about their lives and thought nothing about how their words hurt me. Regardless, I had to forgive, so that I could move on to the next place in life that God was preparing for me.

These are some heartbreaking memories, but they all had to be a part of my story. When all of these scenarios were at play in my life, God knew that one day, I would be telling my story to help inspire others. We each have a story to tell. I had to go through some very tough struggles throughout my life. I had to deal with major heartbreaks and challenges to get to this place I now enjoy.

All my struggles point to the title of this book, *Built to Overcome*. If I hadn't ever dealt with a broken me, a broken man, and a broken marriage; I wouldn't know the joy of what was to come. I wouldn't know the true self love and self-worth that I have today. I thought I didn't matter, but I eventually found my voice. I now know beyond any doubt that I have a purpose in this world. I know my own strength, and I help other women discover and walk in their purpose. You realize just how strong you are when you go through trials and "overcome" them! Which is why I can proclaim, '*I am Built to Overcome*' because God says that I am. I'm glad that I finally came into agreement with Him.

"And they overcame Him by the blood of the Lamb and by the word of their testimony, and they did not love lives to the death." Revelations 12:11 (NKJV)

My Darkest Hour

The news is in... I need surgery! I am scared, terrified, horrified, and any other word that comes to mind when you think of fear! Here I am, almost 30, facing surgery. As you may have guessed, I've never had surgery before. I don't know what to expect. I don't want to do it, BUT I want this pain to go away. It's all on me! Do I have the surgery? Should I not have the surgery? Do I pray this cyst heals and never comes back again? God, I need Your guidance because my fear is getting the best of me.

The surgeon strongly suggests surgery to get the core of the cyst out so it will never grow back again. After praying and speaking with family and friends, I agreed to the surgery. I had to trust whatever God's will is for me, it will be done!

It's surgery day, and I'm in a panic. Even though my blood pressure isn't showing it, the hospital staff helped me to calm down by telling me jokes. They were a breath of fresh air! When they started the medicine through my IV, it put me to sleep, and that was a blessing. Now, all I have to do is wake up from the surgery. As I began counting backwards from 10 the blessed quietness of sleep hit and then there was PEACE. Ten, nine, eighhhhhh… and I'm out!

I woke up to Terrell saying, "I didn't think you were ever going to wake up!" "Wow, he really sounded concerned," I thought. Did I tell him I have a low tolerance for drugs thanks to the DNA contribution from my father? I must have been out for a long while.

I came through the surgery problem-free, and it seemed to be successful. But my PAIN was ridiculous. It was the worst pain I had ever experienced in my life. The surgeon came in to look at the incision. He asked me about my pain level. On a scale of 1 to 10, I told him that my pain was an 8. I should have said a 10 because that is what it felt like. They discharged me a couple of hours after the surgery.

According to my discharge instructions, someone was to monitor me for the next 24 hours. The doctor stated I wasn't to be left alone for any reason. Those first 24 hours after surgery were the absolute worst. The anesthesia made me sick to my stomach and caused me to vomit a lot. Terrell was no help whatsoever. Yeah, he kept an eye on me but did not truly take care of me. He had me throwing up in a 5-gallon work bucket. I was having a whole conversation in my head. "Really Terrell! This is how you treat your wife, the woman you said is the love of your life." It disgusted me that I had to depend on him. "Tell me why I did this to myself, again?" After the pain subsided a little and in between throwing up, I thought, "I can't believe this?! This man has me puking in a 5-gallon work bucket." Realization dawned. For the first time in my life, I had to depend on this man, and I didn't like it.

Terrell must have forgotten the doctor's orders. The morning after my surgery, he decided he would go to our church and cut the grass as he often did. Honestly, I don't think he forgot the doctor's orders. It was more like he didn't care. Over the next few days, it became painfully obvious that he wasn't interested in caring for me. As that truth slapped me upside my head while breaking my heart, I experienced some of the darkest days of my life.

My mind honed in on the thought that he wasn't going to take care of me. From one thought to the next, I began to question everything about our relationship and why I put myself in this position. He is supposed to be my husband, and I'm his wife! Less than 24 hours ago I had surgery. What is he thinking!? Cutting the grass? I'm still under a 24-hour watch. "Yep, he just walked out the house!?!" I thought incredulously. I asked myself, "Is cutting the grass more important than making sure nothing goes wrong with me, your wife?" Confusion set in and I thought, "When did cutting grass become a priority over making sure your wife is taken care of? Under the circumstance, I am sure they can find someone else to cut the grass this one time!"

As he was preparing to leave, I reminded him I'm not supposed to be left alone for the first 24 hours. His response angered me even more, if that was possible, when he said, "I told Deacon and Paul I would help them cut the grass today." As if that made everything alright! It wasn't even all about what he said, but how he said it. He nonchalantly spoke those words as if he did not have anything better to do anyway. He walked out the room without seeing me propped up on the bed with my mouth hanging open and tears threatening to spill out of my eyes. I know he heard the tremble in my voice as I attempted to hold back my tears. I was beyond hurt! And then… he was gone. My heart dropped!! Then came the tears!

Before having the surgery, my sister and I restored our relationship, which was a blessing! However, my mother and sister decided to let Terrell step up and take care of me. In hindsight, their concern about overstepping boundaries gave him more credit than he deserved. I wish they would have intervened, showed up unexpectedly, or called to see if there was anything they could do. If they had, they would have heard how miserable I was and would have been there to take care of me. I totally understand their reasons for not stepping in more. They were allowing him to be my husband and to take care of me as husbands should. Unfortunately, that didn't work out in my best interest. Terrell wasn't fulfilling his role as my husband. My darkest hour was getting darker by the minute.

Later that evening, I started feeling terrible. I didn't know what to think or how to describe what I was feeling. It felt like I was shaking inside. I could literally feel myself trembling on the inside of my body. I was so scared! To look at me no one would know what was happening internally. This continued for a couple of hours. Finally, my mother and sister stopped by. Terrell hadn't come back home yet. I told them how I was feeling. They asked me if I wanted to go to the hospital. Initially, I told them I wanted to wait to see if I would start feeling better. As they waited with me, my health continued to decline. They thought it was best if Terrell took me to the hospital.

I called Terrell several times. He didn't answer, nor did he call back. It was about 8pm when he finally came home. I told him what was going on and that I needed to go to the emergency room. His demeanor spoke volumes. He could not care less. I thought, whatever, and asked my sister if she would take me. She said, "We'll let Terrell take you. Just let me know what's going on." We all walked out to our cars together. My mother and sister pulled off. We pulled out after them, headed to the hospital. You would think I was the one who had an attitude, but no! Terrell did. It was written all over his face.

As soon as we pulled off headed to the hospital, he started in on me. The venom in which he spoke broke my heart and took my breath away. After a minute I began focusing in on what he was saying. He let out a barrage of poisonous, hurtful, and heart-shattering words. "Ain't nothing wrong with you! You just don't want me to go bowling with my friends!" I had heard some extremely hurtful and terrible things come from his mouth, but even I was surprised this time.

I was already in a low place and in tremendous pain. Now, I had to hear this from my husband. The tears streamed down my face as the only sign that his words had hit their mark. In painful agony I thought, "There is no way any man who loves his wife would say these things to her." I could literally feel the anger emanating from him. How could he be mad at me for being sick? He was making this all about him! Just like cutting the grass was not a priority, going bowling with his friends should be furthest thing from his mind.

When we got to the hospital, Terrell was walking in front of me. He didn't even bother helping me out of the car. We walked into the emergency room. The registration process was frustrating. It would have been a lot smoother for me if I had a husband who cared about what was going on. But no! As always, Terrell couldn't care less about what was going on with me.

While we were in the waiting room, he was rude, inconsiderate, and insensitive. He paced back and forth and complained about being hungry and cold the entire time. Not one time did he ask me if I needed anything or if he could help me get more comfortable. The insensitivity was driving me insane. I was the one waiting to see a doctor to find out what was wrong with me! But as usual, I was the only one who cared about my comfort, my feelings, and my life, none of which seemed to matter to him.

The surgery I had wasn't in a place that made sitting comfortable. In my best Forrest Gump voice, it was on my "buttocks!" The condition that led to my surgery is called a pilonidal cyst. It is basically a cyst at the tailbone. It was very difficult to sit comfortably. I was sitting in an uncomfortable hospital waiting room with a stitched-up bottom, while having to deal with my unconcerned, rude, insensitive, and disinterested husband.

My pain level had reached ten by the time I was called to a room. All I could think was, "Thank God, I was one step closer to seeing a doctor." As soon as they called my name, Terrell jumped up out of his chair and went towards the nurse who had called me. Not once did Terrell offer to help me get up from the chair or as I waddled to the room. The compassion and comforting touch I needed from him wasn't there.

When the nurse came in for different tests, he would complain about whatever came to mind. It was cold in there, which everyone knows is standard practice for any hospital. The nurses were doing their job while trying to make me as comfortable as possible. For some reason, Terrell was doing his best to get the nurses to pay more attention to him. The nurse brought him a blanket and gave him directions to the hospital's cafeteria. He left without saying a word. He did not ask me if I needed or wanted anything. He simply got up and walked out the same door the nurse had just exited through.

Now, I don't want to come across as being insensitive. I know he needed to be comfortable, too. However, his primary concern should have been my well-being. Terrell's entire demeanor just made me sicker than the infection that was already coursing through my body. Yes, that was the diagnosis after my four-hour emergency room ordeal. I thank God it was caught in time and that it hadn't seeped into my bloodstream. They gave me an IV, antibiotics, and a prescription for a 7-day antibiotic before being released.

The car ride home was just as unbearable as the last few hours in the emergency room. Terrell wasn't talking. I wasn't talking. It seemed like the longest 30 minutes of my life. I felt like I didn't matter to him. I felt helpless and useless. And he didn't seem to care either way.

After going to the doctor every week for about 2 to 3 months, the incision wasn't healing to the doctor's satisfaction. He was concerned about the scar tissue that was preventing one small part of the incision to heal properly. I began to dread going to the doctor. The visits were becoming more painful with each visit. There was a liquid the doctor applied to the incision. I hated it! The minute it hit my skin, it burned like fire.

At one point, the doctor thought the drops were working, but they didn't completely heal the incision. It was looking like I was going to have to have another surgery. The doctor wanted to remove the scar tissue and dead skin around the incision so that it could heal properly. I was not a happy with his suggestion. Between the pain, the incision not healing, and Terrell's attitude, I regretted having the surgery.

In addition to everything I was dealing with at home and the complications from the surgery, I was having issues with my employer. The company I worked for had family medical leave benefits and short-term disability benefits. I qualified for both since I had been a full-time employee for a few years by this time. The family medical leave benefit kept my job secure while I was out recovering, and short-term disability was supposed to keep my paycheck coming. Which was a blessing I thanked God for daily.

Since my doctor was recommending a second surgery, I let them know I was going to be out even longer. That's when things began to take a turn for the worse. I provided the proper documentation from my doctor, but that didn't seem to matter. I had been receiving my pay the entire time I was out of work. Then I started getting direct deposits for one cent. Words can't describe how I was feeling. I was our only source of income. Without my income, things were going to get really bad, really quick.

Bad came, and it came quickly. My job wasn't in jeopardy, but my paychecks were becoming slim to none. I went through several case managers with the short-term disability company before finally getting the matter resolved. After going without a check for about a month, my pay started back as it should. I was glad I had taken care of that situation, but a bigger problem was looming in the distance.

My darkest hour got even darker! Things had continued to get worse with Terrell. In between surgeries one and two, I experienced a darkness that I pray will never happen again. I couldn't take any more of the verbal abuse from Terrell. I couldn't take any more of being treated as if I didn't matter. There was no reason for Terrell to make me feel like a burden or feel worthless.

I told Terrell I wanted him to leave. Of course, he was clueless why. He refused to leave, so I did. I went to live with my mother. I was still in pain, emotionally and physically. I felt unloved by the person who vowed to love me unconditionally. I had sought after and longed for his love, but I never received it.

While staying at my mom's house, I fell into a deep depression. I felt lifeless. Even though there was daylight shining through the windows, everything around me looked dingy, gloomy, dull, and dark. I felt lifeless and empty. I was in a dark place mentally, emotionally, psychologically, and spiritually.

I was devoted to a marriage and honoring a man who did not care whether I lived or died. My marriage was beyond repair, and I took it personally. I turned on myself. My self-esteem spiraled. I made space for Terrell in my life. I poured everything I had to give into our relationship, and he threw it up in my face. Like a vampire, he sucked the life out of me, and I had to stop the bleeding. I could not live like this anymore. I was barely hanging on by a thread.

I was at my breaking point. What was the point? Maybe I should just end it all. I constantly asked myself, "What is it going to be? Am I going to live, or die?" My life up to this point hadn't been peaches and cream, but it had been a lot better than what I was experiencing with Terrell.

I called my best friend, Shelly and my sister. They came to Mom's house, and I shared with them everything that had happened between myself and Terrell, and that I had left him. After spilling my guts, neither of them were happy with Terrell. I needed to heal, get my life back on track, and decide what to do about my marriage. That required me to have a safe place to land. We decided I would stay with my sister for a while.

I couldn't share with her the depth of my hurt nor how close I was to committing suicide. I told my sister I was feeling shaky again and that everything just looked dark. I was afraid to close my eyes to go to sleep. Everything seemed to have a dark cloud around it. I felt like I was walking in the valley of the shadow of death. My sister prayed for me that night. She prayed one of those mighty prayers over me. Her prayer was so powerful, I could feel life coming back into my body. I felt more peace than I had felt in days, and I went to sleep shortly thereafter. Hallelujah!

The next day Terrell was on the phone, acting like he didn't understand why I left. There was no fight left in me as I held the phone and listened to him try to back pedal because he knew he really messed up this time. I was at the point where nothing he said could convince me that he cared about me. Yeah, I know! What was I thinking? Why, in God's name, did I give him another chance and go back home?

The second surgery came and went. It seemed to be a success. I was healing as expected. Two months later, I was released by my doctor to return to work.

Terrell and I started talking about buying a home. He had been active in church from the beginning of our relationship. He had recently started taking part in various ministries. It seemed as if the teachings and the relationships he had formed were finally getting through to him. For the first time in a very long time, he was working a steady job and helping to pay the bills. I thought this would be a great time to take things to the next level.

The conversations we were having were making sense. Terrell was keeping his word for the first time in a very long time. He started to take our marriage seriously, and I decided to take him at his word. I didn't want to go through a divorce. I really wanted our marriage to work. I had prayed a million prayers regarding our marriage over the years, and figured this was the time God answered them.

We were approved for a home loan, and I was over the moon with excitement. I had lived in apartments my whole life and having a home of our own was a dream come true. I was the first one in my immediate family to be a homeowner.

I loved everything about the house we chose, except the driveway and the backyard. It had a garage, so that made up for what I didn't like. I wasn't too picky, being that it was in a great area. The inside was more than I could ever dream of having. For once in our marriage, everything seemed good. Would it stay that way, or was it just the calm before yet another storm?

We moved into our new home and got settled. It was a lease to own deal, but I still couldn't believe that it was ours. I was overjoyed! As the saying goes, everything that glitters ain't gold. From the outside looking in, we looked like a loving and happy couple enjoying our first home. However, the cracks in our foundation would soon become visible. My newfound happiness soon turned into despair. I was committed to Terrell for better or worse. And things were about to take a turn for the worse.

We were living in what I thought was our dream home, but it wasn't a happy home. There was a lot of hurt there. It was cold, sad, and lonely! I was by myself a lot. We weren't a happy couple, and the air between us was so thick you could choke on it. Yeah, I had my big, pretty house on the hill, but I didn't have the love I so desperately longed for.

We were not financially prepared to move into that house. As always, I took the back seat in the decision making. I had followed Terrell's lead. Big mistake! I was left with the financial responsibility that comes along with the house on the hill. In what I thought was a great financial investment, I had taken a large chunk of my annual bonus for the down payment on our dream home, a decision I came to regret.

I was searching for a little piece of happiness I could bring into our marriage. Unfortunately, my efforts were in vain. I was married. However, if I didn't do it (whatever it was), it didn't get done. I took on all the roles of the marriage. Terrell wasn't doing the things I thought husbands were supposed to do, like work to provide for our family, and love, respect, and cherish their wives. I had to assume my role as a wife and do his part when he was slacking and unreliable.

At this point in the marriage, I was ready to leave. I couldn't take it anymore. I was sick and tired of being sick and tired. I wanted better. I wasn't happy. I didn't feel loved. My love and my efforts were being taken for granted. I wanted to wash my hands of the insanity, the hurt, the pain, and the uncertainty. If that meant leaving Terrell, then that's just what I was going to do. I knew there was better, but I wasn't sure if I had the strength to leave in search of the better, I deserved.

Within three months of moving into my dream home, I was apartment hunting. I filled out application after application for an apartment. They denied me for all of them. Early in our relationship, I would have been approved for any apartment. However, after our marriage, my credit score declined. In fact, it went from good to terrible. Everything was in my name, so all the late payments, non-payments, and write offs had destroyed my credit. It didn't look like they would approve me for an apartment. I had to stay and figure things out. I began wondering why God wouldn't let me out of the marriage.

I stayed, but I didn't believe Terrell would change. Things remained the same over the next three months. Then came the big news. We were pregnant. SURPRISE! When I found out we were pregnant, I understood why all of those apartment applications had been denied. I took this great news as God giving us a second chance to work on our marriage and make things better. He is a God of second, third, and fourth chances, right? Surely, Terrell would change once our bundle of joy arrived, right?

When I found out we were pregnant, I told myself that I would try to work things out. I vowed to work on our marriage for the sake of the little bundle of joy who was on the way. I knew what it was like being raised in a single-parent household, and I wanted better for my child. I wanted our baby to have so much more than what I had as a child. I wanted his/her life to be the best it could be, and I was going to do everything in my power to make sure that happened.

Well, Terrell made sure it was going to be easier said than done. There was another big development that came along with the pregnancy news. Terrell got released from his job. We were experiencing some intense times in our marriage once again.

I did everything possible to keep us in that house, but we were so far behind in the payments. Terrell tried to help by speaking with the lender. But his way of handling business was to curse everybody out. As a result, the lender didn't want to deal with us anymore. We got kicked out of our lease to own house.

We were pregnant and packing up the house. We moved back to the same apartments we had just moved from a few months prior. That was heartbreaking for me. I felt like I had finally accomplished something great with that house. Now, I had lost it all. I had been allowed to taste living in a beautiful home, only to have it taken away from me. It could have been avoided, but Terrell didn't consider my feelings, thoughts, needs, or desires, yet again!

Our excitement paled in light of us losing our home. Although I was devastated, I made the best out of the situation. We were able to return to the apartment complex with no problems. I focused on the silver lining. At least we had somewhere to go.

I took a day off work to help pack up our belongings. Why did I do that? I had to listen to Terrell tell me I should have gone to work because I was in his way. I was pregnant and nauseous. I was carrying his child. I had to pack up and downsize from a 3-bedroom house to a 1-bedroom apartment because he wasn't taking care of his business. Yet all I heard about was being in his way.

Once again, I allowed the tears to fall. I overcame the silent cry quickly. There was a lot of work to be done, and I had to suck up the tears in a hurry. I couldn't let him see my tears, or I would really have to listen to a mouthful of harsh words. It would have made a bad situation even worse.

I was in a tough place. I was married, but I felt like I was going at life all alone. I loved our house and hated the thought of having to leave it. Of course, I thought about what people would say about us. I was going to miss my garage most of all. I had dreamed about having my garage door opener in my car and driving right in with the press of a button. That was a first for me, and it made me feel all warm and fuzzy inside. I felt like I had accomplished something great. Now, I had to leave it all behind.

I blamed Terrell. If he had not pushed me into thinking bigger in that moment, I probably would not have gotten the house. I was mad at him because he didn't hold up his end of the bargain by getting and keeping a good job. We didn't go in blind. Terrell knew how much money I made. I'm sure he felt like I would be able to continue to take care of us, even with the increase in our expenses. I don't believe he had any intentions of helping me with the load of owning a house for long. He worked just long enough to make me think he had my back. In all actuality, I should have been the one having his back. I should have been able to depend on him. Now, I had to accept my firstborn child would be brought home to an apartment instead of a beautiful house.

We had been married for five years when we found out we were pregnant. My first trimester was horrible. It was my first pregnancy, so I wasn't sure what to expect. I had heard the stories, but it's not quite the same when you're experiencing it. Morning sickness turned into all day sickness. I was miserable day in and day out, yet I was so excited to be carrying my first bundle of joy.

There is nothing like hearing the doctor tell you, 'You're pregnant.' It's an amazing thing to feel your child moving in your belly for the very first time. I can't describe it in words. It is something I will never forget. I felt flutters here and there around the end of my third month. The biggest kick came when I was eating ice cream. I remember thinking, "My baby has a sweet tooth!" That wasn't surprising. I love sweets, too!

Five months into my pregnancy, I felt better. I was getting regular checkups, and all was going well with our bundle of joy. I didn't get sick at the smell of certain foods and fragrances anymore. But some smells still made me nauseous. I remember telling my sissy pooh not to wear a certain fragrance around me. It just made me feel yucky. I'm so glad she isn't easily offended because I am sure it didn't roll off my tongue smoothly.

I remember my excitement around the ultrasound to determine our baby's gender. I couldn't wait to find out what we were having. I wanted a girl, and Terrell wanted a boy. The ultrasound technician had to try hard to get our little rascal to cooperate. The baby was a busy body that day. The tech would go to one side of my belly, and the baby would move to the other side. Finally, we saw it. We're having a boy! We were able to get some good pictures of him with his hand on his forehead, as if to say we were bothering him. It seemed like he just wanted to be left alone. It was so funny and one of the most memorable moments of my pregnancy.

I wish all of my pregnancy memories were happy. Unfortunately, there were some painful memories. Near the end of my pregnancy, I cried more than I smiled. The most painful moment happened when I was 8 months pregnant. I remember it so clearly. I was getting ready for work, and I was an emotional wreck. I was beyond huge, and. I couldn't see my feet. Bending down to reach my feet was not an option.

As I sat on the bed struggling, Terrell came out of the bathroom. I asked him to help me put on my shoes. Terrell looked at me with disgust. He didn't say a word. He just turned around, walked out of the bedroom, and left the apartment.

Although I heard the door close, I was thinking this was some kind of a joke. In my mind, I wanted to believe he didn't just walk out and totally ignore me. Surely, he was just going to the car to get something and coming right back. Sadly, that wasn't the case. He didn't come back. I couldn't believe he would not help me with something as simple as putting on my shoes. I couldn't believe the man to whom I had said "I do" didn't have enough respect or common decency to even respond to me. Where was the love? My darkest hour turned into hours!

Once again, I had to conceal my hurt and my emotions. I knew I couldn't stop working because I needed medical care. We were about to have a hospital stay, and we needed the insurance to pay for that. Plus, our baby would need medical care. I *had* to go to work. No ifs, ands, or buts about it! So, I "sucked it up" and put on my shoes. Was this really my life?

During my last trimester, I was mad at Terrell more than I was happy with him. I prayed to God, and I covered our baby with prayer daily because I knew the baby could pick up on what the mother was feeling. I didn't want any of my emotions to have a negative impact on our baby. I didn't want our child to feel any of my unstable emotions. When I was feeling sad or mad, I would ask God to protect the baby.

My relationship with Terrell was so unstable. There were parts of me that still loved him. Some days were good, and some days were horrible. I was growing more tired and weary as time passed, but I was still trying to hold on to the marriage. I didn't want to raise my son as a single mother.

Perhaps Terrell would shape up and do better once our child was born. Surely, he could see past his own selfishness to do what was best for our family. I hoped our son would cause a change in him. Only time would tell if that would be the case.

A Deeper Look…

When Terrell walked out of the house like he didn't hear me asking for help with my shoes, it hurt me beyond repair (or so I thought). Is this really happening? Is this a joke? Am I being punked? Unfortunately, this was really my life! My husband just ignored me and walked out on me as if I had said nothing. How am I supposed to feel after this?

I couldn't believe how Terrell had treated me during my pregnancy or after my surgery. This was the same man who would tell me he loved me repeatedly. He would even say that he was happy he met me. And, just like turning on a light in a dark room, he would switch from words of love to degrading and destructive words. Why then? Why now? Especially during one of the most difficult times of my life. Once again, he simply turned his back on me and left me to handle the situation all by myself.

What was happening? What went wrong? What did I do to deserve this?

I began feeling like I had gotten myself into this mess, and I was the only person who could get me out of it. So, I pushed my feelings way deep down inside and suffered in silence. This entire ordeal taught me a valuable lesson. I needed to have people in my life with whom I can be open, honest, and free. Especially since God doesn't expect anyone to go through life alone.

I had gotten good at hiding my feelings and making everyone think everything was going well. You know how we put on the fake smile while wearing a mask to hide the truth? I was masking my problems and my pain, and I only made things worse. Covering up my hurt would continue to be an ongoing cycle of devastation for me. Only God could help me break the cycle.

God blessed me with a praying sister. She's a mighty prayer warrior who prays with conviction and expectation. I don't know if I would have emerged from my state of depression without her prayers. We have grown extremely close over the years, and I thank God for all that she adds to my life. God knew I would need her! He is a good, good, good Father!

I still wonder why I let Terrell back in after going through my depression. I didn't give myself enough time to analyze and process everything, but it was all a part of God's plan for my life. This time had to happen! My 'Darkest Hour' had to happen!

Losing our house and moving back into an apartment was a trying time for me. I was going to miss the idea of becoming a homeowner. What I didn't know then, but know now is that, as with most things in my life, I almost allowed that house to define me. Jesus saw the path I was on, and before pride could set in, it was taken away.

I hadn't yet learned how to free myself from people and the words that they said about me. Truth is, we all have a story to tell, and we all go through tough times. I didn't know who I was, so it didn't take much for me to grab hold and attach myself to material things to soothe the pain of not loving myself or knowing my worth. I would hold on for dear life, as if it couldn't get any better than that present thing or situation. I was holding on to that house for dear life because I thought I had "arrived." I didn't think I could come back from the loss. I felt like I would never become a homeowner after losing that house. That thought and many others would prove yet another lie that I told myself.

My attachment to people was another hurdle I had to overcome. Everyone doesn't come into your life to stay. Sometimes they come to teach you a lesson or two. Ecclesiastes 3:1 (NKJV) says it best, *"To everything there is a season, A time for every purpose under the heaven."* People are sometimes seasonal! God sends some people into your life to create lifetime relationships. While others are only there for a moment or a season. Learning to differentiate between them is imperative. I learned that the hard way. I have always felt when people come into my life, they are supposed to stay. That definitely is not the case!

My faith and trust in God were being stretched and strengthened. I wasn't where I wanted to be in God, but I was striving to get there daily. I know without any doubt that HE is my savior and not once did He ever leave me. His words are true! *"For He Himself said, I will never leave you nor forsake you."* Romans 13:5 (NKJV)

When we are at our worst, God is still at His best. HE is determined to get us to our expected end. *"For I know the thoughts that I think toward you, says the Lord, thoughts of peace and not of evil, to give you a future and a hope."* Jeremiah 29:11 (NKJV)

I look back on these moments and wonder how in the world did I not lose my mind. The only answer is GOD! HE is a way-maker, a mind regulator, and HE will always see us through. When we don't think there is a way, HE will make a way out of no way! I have often said and heard other people say, God is my strength. It seems I used those words so loosely, without ever thinking about what I was saying. When I use those words now, there is new meaning behind them. I could easily be somewhere crazy and not even know my name. With all I've endured, I could be strung out on drugs and/or in the crazy house…. BUT GOD! He truly is my strength, and He has helped me to overcome every obstacle that has been placed in my path. Only God gets the credit for helping me overcome my self-esteem issues and lack of self-love. Did I ever doubt and second guess myself and Him? You better believe and know that I did. But the God I serve is faithful. He was always there.

I had some hard pills to swallow. I had some tough lessons to learn up to this point in my marriage. And my sad truth is that this chapter of my life wasn't over yet.

My Voice of Reason

I had been in labor for about 12 hours when the doctor came in and said, "The baby's heart rate is going up and down. He's in distress, so we're going to have to go in and take him!" That was not the news I wanted to hear! My mind went to all the bad things that could happen to me or the baby. I didn't have time to think about what would happen next. I was about to have a c-section.

We had been praying for a healthy delivery and a healthy baby. God answered our prayers. We didn't have any complications with the delivery. My voice of reason arrived at 4:34 pm, healthy and weighing 8 pounds and 2 ounces. Javeon was total excellence! Our bright-eyed, handsome bundle of joy came out kicking and screaming! My life changed as soon as I laid eyes on him.

Having my first child was a whirlwind of an experience. The first few weeks of Javeon's life were challenging but joyful. I enjoyed every moment with him. I was amazed by our miracle of life.

After my eight-week recovery period, I had to face reality. My maternity leave was ending, so I had to return to work. Staying home with Javeon would have been nice, but someone had to pay the bills. I was abundantly blessed because my mother was able to take care of Javeon when I returned to work. That was an extra expense I really couldn't afford. Knowing my son was with my mother, instead of at a daycare, made my days at work much easier.

After my return to work, things continued to get worse in my marriage. I had expected Terrell to man up and do what was best for his family, but that was wishful thinking on my part. It was amazing to me how he could get a job so easily, then quickly lose it. Terrell had many skills and talents, but his attitude would get him in trouble and ultimately fired from almost every job. Once Javeon was born, I thought he would work on becoming a better person at least on the job. Unfortunately, that didn't happen, either.

I really didn't like my job, but it paid well. It helped me take care of my new bundle of joy, so I had to stay. I couldn't quit. I couldn't have the same luxuries as Terrell did when it came to working and taking care of a family. Now, there was someone in addition to myself I had to live for.

Three o'clock in the morning became Terrell's magic number. On the nights he stayed out late, he would usually walk through the door at 3:00 am. I never had any solid proof he was cheating, but I suspected that's what he was doing. What else could he have been doing at three o'clock in the morning? I finally got up the nerve to ask him what he was doing until three in the morning. He told me he was "spending time with God." Wonderful! We all need to do that! But isn't God at our house, too?

He went on to say he needed to be outside to feel at peace and to get some fresh air. Wouldn't it be great if he talked to God at a respectable hour? Instead, I was left pacing the floor and crying at night. I had to wonder where he was, what he was doing, whether he's hurt, or if he's somewhere cheating.

I heard comments, and I saw text messages between Terrell and a single female church member. I questioned him about her. His response was he was just listening to her talk about her problems with her boyfriend. Really? Did I hear him correctly? Our marriage is barely hanging on, but he's helping another female with her relationship problems! I got to a point where I realized and accepted Javeon deserved to have at least one parent who cared enough for him to do right by him and had his best interests at heart.

Because of our stressful marriage issues, I knew I was not emotionally and mentally stable. I wasn't clear on who I was or what I was doing with my life, and something had to change. I had to get better and stay better for myself and Javeon.

In the early months of Javeon's life, I began to think more about our future. I wanted… no; I deserved better! I decided I was going to change my focus from fixing our marriage to bettering myself to be a better mother for Javeon. Things were about to change. Things had to change! And those changes were going to take place quickly.

I had dealt with a lot from Terrell prior to having Javeon, but the struggles I had endured wouldn't become his struggles. I was determined to make sure of that. I had been through hell and back with Terrell, but I would not allow Javeon to go through that. No way! No how! If not for me, then for him. If I couldn't find the strength to live better for myself, my voice of reason was now here. Life was going to get better. It had to!

My job had a lot of opportunities for advancement, but I wasn't sure if I qualified. They offered a very generous package for continuing education, so I went back to school to pursue a college degree. I thought if I was going to stay at that company, I should at least attempt to get a higher paying position. Getting a degree would help me achieve that goal. So, I began my journey to become a college graduate. My mother became my constant support system. She supported me as I sought a degree and kept Javeon when I was in class and needed to study. I wouldn't have been able to make it happen without her.

I also wanted Javeon to have a backyard to play in. I worked extremely hard to fix my credit. I got my score high enough to buy my very first home. An upfront purchase this time, not a lease to own. Great things were still happening amid what seemed like a bad situation! I thanked God for allowing me to be a trailblazer!

I purchased my home when Javeon was 10 months old. We celebrated his first birthday in our first home! It was a dream come true. I was one proud momma! I got to see my baby boy take his first steps in our new home!

While I was trying to build a better life for myself and Javeon, Terrell was still living irresponsibly, going from job to job, and barely contributing to the household bills. While I was going through the home buying process, Terrell got into trouble and went back to jail.

Although Terrell wasn't putting forth his best effort to take care of us, I still didn't want to keep his child from him. I remember taking Javeon to see him while he was in jail. Thankfully, he was in the work camp program because it was cleaner. They were housed separately, and it wasn't as strict as being in the actual jailhouse. I think Javeon was the one thing that kept Terrell positive while he was in jail.

I showed Terrell pictures of our new house, but he didn't seem thrilled about it at all. He made promises of how he would do better once he got out. I didn't know if I could believe him. I would not let that stop me from being the best mom I could be to Javeon. I was overjoyed and excited about my accomplishment. I was also on the path to attaining my business degree. Is this what happiness looks like?

Eventually, Terrell came home from jail. He kept his promises he had made while he was in jail. Unfortunately, it only lasted about a month. Then we were back to our old routine. After they released him from jail, I endured his mess for a year. I couldn't take it anymore... I was fed up! I was at my wit's end, and I needed God to do what only He could do. A change had to come!

While driving home from class one night, I had a long, hard talk with God. I poured my heart out and cried out to Him. I made some demands. "God, you have got to get me out of this marriage," I cried. I pleaded with Him to either get me out of the marriage, or fix it. We were 7 years in, and the number 7 means completion!

I really wanted out. I didn't believe it could be fixed. God has all the power and can fix anything. I cried out to God, saying, "God, if it is in your will that I be free from this marriage, don't let Terrell be there when I get home." I asked God to allow me to pick up Javeon, get home, get inside, and lock the door. "I will know that's You granting me Your permission to be free from this marriage."

God did exactly what I asked Him to do! Terrell wasn't home when Javeon and I got home. I don't think I've ever moved so fast in my life! I got Javeon and our things out of the car and into the house. Then I locked the door and said, "Thank You, Jesus!"

Next, I had to consider what I would say and do when Terrell got home. I was nervous just thinking about what his response might be. I locked the deadbolt because Terrell didn't have a key to the deadbolt lock. When he arrived, he unlocked the doorknob lock, but couldn't get inside. He rang the doorbell. Through the locked door, I told him I didn't want to be in the marriage anymore and I wanted him to leave.

Up to this point, I hadn't shared with anyone that I feared Terrell. Terrell had never actually hit me, but he had displayed threatening behavior. Early in our marriage, there was an incident. We had been arguing about something. Terrell threw a clothes hanger across the room at me and then came running towards me. He jumped on top of me, straddling me on our bed. I cried and yelled for him to get off me. He had my arm pinned down so tightly, causing me to cut my arm on the keys on the bed.

I had reason to be afraid of Terrell. He had a horrible attitude, and he had a lifestyle that included being involved with gangs and people with bad reputations. I knew what he was capable of. He had told me many stories about his past before and during our marriage.

I was nervous and trembling as I talked to him through the door. I was praying the whole time. "God, please just let him leave peacefully," I prayed. I didn't want to have to call the cops. I didn't want Javeon to witness an altercation. I prayed and continued to ask Terrell to leave. After a few minutes, he left. He said he would come back the next day to get his things. I breathed a huge sigh of relief, and I gave God a big "Thank you!" I was relieved the ordeal was over. He had left without putting up a fight, but I was unsure and somewhat afraid of what the next day would bring.

All night I prayed things would remain peaceful when Terrell came to get his things. I didn't want to have to call the police. I hardly slept a wink all night. I listened for any sound that could be him trying to break into the house. My mind was racing with all kinds of crazy thoughts about what he might try to do to harm me.

There was a part of me that thought we should just separate. Maybe we just needed some space to sort things out, I thought. Yet there was a bigger part of me that just wanted to wash my hands and be done with it all. I was tired of the merry go round, the back and forth, and the drama.

I made it through what seemed to be the longest night of my life. The time came for Terrell to come and pick up some things from the house. I wasn't looking forward to it, but I knew it had to be done. I made sure he came when Javeon was with my mother. It wasn't a pleasant experience at all. Terrell became confrontational. He got close to my face, trying to intimidate me. "Why are you doing this," he yelled. I still can't believe he had the nerve to ask why. Where had he been for the last 7 years?

After an ongoing yelling and screaming match, he saw I wasn't going to back down, so he took his things and left. Finally! I was so relieved that part was over. I could rest and breathe a little easier. The separation was needed. I just had to listen to God for my next steps.

Terrell tried to talk me into staying in the marriage several times after our separation. When he realized I wasn't budging, his attitude became horrible. In turn, so did mine. I was tired of him. I was angry about everything he had put me through. I was even more upset with myself for allowing him to mistreat me for seven years.

As a last-ditch effort, Terrell asked me to go to counseling. "Really? Now you're suggesting counseling?" I thought. I had talked to Terrell several times about going to counseling before. Terrell agreed, and we went to counseling with two different pastors. His attitude was beyond ridiculous both times. He didn't even attempt to change his unimaginable ways. Although I wanted to say no, I figured I could give it one more try.

We were counseled by a special couple whom we both loved, adored, and admired. They were Javeon's godparents, so they were rooting for us. They wanted nothing but to see us to stay together. However, they were on the outside looking in. I knew what I had gone through, and I knew what I would not go through any longer. That wasn't an option, regardless of what was said. I had a made-up mind, and only God Himself could change it.

I already knew what was to come. Remember that night that I cried out to God on my way home from school? God had given me an answer. I was certain about what I was going to do next, and I had made my peace with God about it. I still had my eyes and ears open because I didn't want to miss any signs from God. I was listening closely to hear His voice every step of the way.

Once again, Terrell didn't make any changes after counseling. However, he tried pulling at my heartstrings. He would call and tell me he was sleeping in his truck. My heart would sink every single time, but I couldn't let him get the best of me. I had to remember what had transpired over the past seven years. I had to think about Javeon's life and what could happen if I allowed Terrell to stay in it.

Each time I would see Terrell, he seemed to look worse. He would call me to ask if he could take a shower at the house. I hated it, but I had to tell him no. If we would no longer be together, I couldn't allow him access to my home. My heart was hurting for him, but I had to stand my ground. That's just the way it had to be. If I loosened up just an inch, he could wiggle back into my life.

Divorce was my next move. My mother, sister, close friends, and my Pastor were who I sought wise counsel from. Once I retained a divorce attorney, I moved forward with the divorce proceedings. If I am being honest, I didn't know how to feel about everything. Although I felt at peace with my decision, a piece of me hurt for Terrell.

I always saw the good in a person, even if they've shown me nothing but the bad. That's just the way God made me. Terrell would tell me I had to get punched in the face or hit with a brick before I realized someone was doing me wrong. It's funny how often HE was that "someone."

About six months into our separation, I received a call from Terrell. He was crying. He told me he was in the hospital. His kidneys had failed. He needed a kidney transplant, or he was going to have to be on dialysis for the rest of his life. My heart sank, and thoughts flooded my mind. I couldn't believe what I was hearing!

GOD! What do I do now? Why is this happening now? Terrell was still my husband at this point. Terrell still had a soul inside of him that needed nurturing. He couldn't go through this ordeal alone! Wait.... we're going through a divorce. Pam, you've already started the process. But are you really going to divorce your sick husband?

All the thoughts a caring wife would think after getting that call were running through my mind. I couldn't believe what was happening, and I didn't know what to do. My heart stopped for a split second after hearing the news. What am I to do? This could change everything!

After I hung up the phone, I had to just be still and let it all sink into my mind. I was shocked! God, what are You doing? Can I really go through with the divorce now? Wouldn't that make me the meanest, cruelest person in the world? How would Javeon react when he's older, and he realizes the circumstances of our divorce? Will he understand? Terrell is the father of my child. Is this really happening right now?

Since our separation, I had been feeling better than I felt in years. I prayed daily for direction. I asked God to give me a sign if He didn't want me to proceed with the divorce. God never gave me a sign to stop the process, so I continued with the divorce.

The date of our court hearing arrived. I met my attorney at our scheduled time. Terrell was representing himself. The judge asked Terrell if he agreed with the divorce. Terrell replied, "No, because I have Stage 4 kidney disease." When I got on the stand, the judge asked me several questions regarding our marriage. He asked me if I wanted to save my marriage. My heart dropped just a little when I heard myself say, "No." For once, I was starting to value myself. My feelings matter. My voice matters. I matter. It was finally sinking in!

It was all over. I walked out of the courtroom so happy! I had to do my happy dance. My heart was rejoicing. I had been set free. My sister said, *"I ain't never seen nobody so happy to be getting a divorce!"*

A few months passed, and I didn't hear from Terrell. I knew he was upset with me, but I was okay with that. After all he put me through; I was just glad I made it out! I had overcome!

Javeon was only three years old at the time of the divorce. He hadn't really seen much of his dad before the divorce. Terrell hadn't established a deep connection with Javeon. After the divorce, Terrell would rarely call or visit, so Javeon would think about him and miss him. I would always give him my phone and allow him to call his dad.

Terrell was missing out on getting to know God's special gift to us, Javeon. I knew he could do a lot better with calling and visiting Javeon, but I wouldn't complain about Terrell in front of Javeon. I wanted Javeon to develop his own opinion of his dad and not be persuaded by anything he heard me say.

There was one thing I commended Terrell for doing. He would always tell Javeon, "I want you to be better than me. I want you to be a better man than I am." I appreciated him for that. Javeon heard from his dad's mouth that he could be better and do better in his life.

After our divorce, Terrell was in and out of the hospital over the next few years. His health continued to decline. I don't think he took his condition seriously. He didn't seem to take care of himself like he needed to. Terrell wasn't even going to dialysis like he was supposed to. I think he just didn't care anymore. He appeared to be giving up on life.

One morning Terrell called me. He was crying, and I could hardly understand what he was saying. Terrell said that the surgeon was coming to talk to him about having open heart surgery. There could be benefits, but there were also some serious risks with the surgery. The doctors had given him some grim statistics. He had a 30% chance of surviving the surgery.

I asked Terrell if he wanted me to bring Javeon to see him. He would always say he wanted to get a little better first. I told Javeon his dad was sick, but I never went into the details of his condition. I felt for him, but I couldn't be there for him. I hated the fact he didn't have anyone who cared enough to be there during this time.

Although the odds were stacked against him, Terrell proceeded with the surgery. There were complications during and after the surgery. Things went downhill quickly. Unfortunately, Terrell passed away. I was so sorry to hear Terrell had lost his battle. I hated Terrell didn't let Javeon come to see him before things took a turn for the worse.

My voice of reason was why I had to remove Terrell from my life. Now, my heart was hurting because I had to tell my voice of reason the bad news. Javeon was seven years old. He wasn't old enough to understand, but I knew it would hurt him. Although he didn't see his dad often, he always enjoyed seeing him when he did. Now, I had to tell him his dad was gone.

Terrell's family was handling the funeral arrangements. They contacted me to get information on Javeon for the obituary. They also asked if I had any pictures of Terrell for the obituary. I had recently thrown away my pictures of Terrell, including our wedding pictures. They would have to get pictures from someone else. The decision I made to throw the pictures of Terrell away was a selfish one. As I look back now, I realize those pictures could have helped Javeon remember his dad. Someday, he may ask to see pictures of his mom and dad. What will I have to show him? For that reason, I hated I threw away those pictures.

As I sat through Terrell's funeral, I was sad about how his life ended. Although he had his struggles, I had hoped someday he would overcome them. I found peace in knowing God has a reason and a plan for everything.

In the days and months following Terrell's death, Javeon would cry when he missed his dad. Certain songs that reminded him of his dad would make him cry. I encouraged Javeon to just let it out. I didn't want him to bottle-up his emotions. I didn't want him to become angry, bitter, or sick from holding in his grief.

Thankfully, those grief-filled times didn't last. Javeon is doing well, and I am so very grateful for the young man he's becoming. Terrell would be proud. Terrell, he *is* going to be a better man than you were, just like you always told him to be! Thank you for the lifelong lessons you shared with him. What you shared will be in his heart forever.

A Deeper Look…

I thought the birth of our son would spark a change in Terrell. However, I was wrong. Things didn't get better. In fact, they got worse.

It's never a good sign when a married man is consistently out at 3am without his wife, unless he has a 3rd shift job. The times Terrell came home at 3am were some of the most trying times in my life. The actions Terrell displayed daily spoke nothing of love. My many pleas for him to stop disrespecting me by coming home at 3 o'clock in the morning were ignored. I realized my tears no longer mattered to him.

Terrell had hurt me time and time again with his disrespectful actions and verbal abuse over the years. He didn't care that his actions were hurting me, and he showed no interest in changing his behavior. My feelings were being crushed by the one who said he would love me as Christ loves the Church!

I think what gave me the courage to walk away from the marriage was when I realized I had accepted Terrell's abuse at the cost of my own mental health and stability. That wasn't the only thing I took from the marriage. I lost hope in the institution of marriage. I lost sight of my identity and my worth. I was at my lowest. How I felt on the inside showed on the outside as well. While wallowing in self-pity, I let myself go.

Ladies, we all know how we are about our hair and our clothes, jewelry, makeup- you know the things that make us feel good. Well, I had lost the desire for all of that. Had I really allowed a man to drag me down that far? But this wasn't just any man. We're talking about my husband, the man who stood before God and took vows to love and cherish me. Sadly, he wasn't doing any of it. Obviously, he didn't take his vows seriously enough to care or even notice there was a big problem!

I experienced lack in many areas, especially my attire. It made me sad because I loved shopping and wearing the cutest clothes possible. I loved matching my jewelry and handbags with my outfits. But my child always had to come first. He had everything he needed.

I didn't have a lot growing up, but when I started working, I put more care into how I carried myself. I cared about the clothes I wore and making sure everything matched. I started making sure my hair was done, and that I had the cutest outfits my check could afford. I would even get my nails done as often as I could. The more and more I stopped caring about my life, the more and more it showed up in my appearance.

The saying 'I can do bad all by myself' is the truth! It has become a truth I live my life by. As I took the journey to know Pam, I had to forgive myself for allowing a man, even my husband, to bring me down. Proverbs 18:22 tells us that a wife brings favor into the husband's life when she is treated as a gift from God. When the wife is not seen or treated as God designed, it impacts not only her personally but also the generations she is to birth. Sometimes it even impacts how or if she shares her gifts with the world. Don't allow a man or anyone else to bring you down. You matter and the gifts that are within you are needed in this world. God gave them to you for you to release in this earth.

When I was at my lowest, I did not believe I was a gift, nor did I believe I have anything to offer the world. My life took a downward spiral, and I didn't care anymore. Internally, I was beyond broken. Externally, I wore my hurt like garment I put on daily.

As I think back on a conversation with a guy at work, I can see instances where my despair showed in my choice of clothing. We were getting ready for our supervisor to come in for a team meeting when he told me my outfit "looks like a sweat suit." I reacted in the worst way, mainly because my feelings were hurt and because he said it loud enough for everyone in the meeting to hear. The nearest crack on the floor was where I wanted to melt. I was hurt, embarrassed, and mad. I felt this was all Terrell's fault, and most of it was. If he had been working and bringing in an income, everything wouldn't be on my plate. I could shop again. I didn't even know what shopping felt like anymore because I couldn't do everything I could do for myself before having Javeon. As his mother, it is my responsibility to put Javeon's needs first. Truth be told, I didn't have the strength to care anymore, but I didn't want everyone else to know I didn't care. Oxymoron, right?!

Besides looking like hot mess, my hair was going through "growing pains" as well. I took pride in my hair. It was as long as it had ever been, and it was finally healthy. I made sure I got my hair done every two weeks, like clockwork. One day, as my stylist was doing my hair, she said, "What did you do? Has anyone else been doing your hair?" I said, "No, I don't let anyone do my hair but you." She said, "You have two bald spots!" I was devastated! Nothing in my life had changed or was changing other than all the problems I was having with Terrell. My husband had stressed me out so badly my hair broke off, causing bald spots. When I say bald spots, they were as smooth as a baby's bottom in two different areas on my scalp. My stylist told me the areas where I lost my hair could be hidden. My hair was long enough to hide the areas, so it wouldn't be noticeable. It was another moment where God's grace saved the day.

One of my breaking points came when a dear friend of mine pulled me aside one day after church. "What's wrong with you?" she asked. As I looked puzzled, she said I wasn't taking care of myself like before. She noted my hair, my clothes, and my demeanor had changed. "You're not the same, Pam, and you just don't look happy. You seem like you just don't care anymore," she continued.

It's good to have true friends in your life who notice when something is off about you. They come to you with genuine concern, not just wanting to know the tea about what's happening in your life. I trusted her enough to tell her my marriage was in shambles, and I was trying to figure out how to pull myself back together again.

That was an eye opener for me. It was a subtle reminder from God I wasn't myself anymore. I had lost the little bit of myself I had known. I was no longer Pam. I wasn't living. I was merely existing. I was hanging on by a thread that at any moment was about to break. I couldn't allow that to happen.

I was married to someone who blatantly disrespected me in words and actions. He showed me over and over that he couldn't care less about me. I already had self-esteem issues. Then I believed even more that I really didn't matter! Low self-esteem became negative self-esteem.

Time would prove that Terrell treated me how I allowed him to treat me. I had to value myself enough to set standards for myself. I knew I couldn't deviate from those standards and still feel a sense of self-worth.

When I think about the mental anguish that Terrell caused me, I thank God for keeping me through the storms. God kept me from losing my mind. Even though I felt lost in the marriage, He helped me to find myself during and after the process.

One of the many lessons I learned from Terrell is you can't give what you don't have, and you can't give what was never given. Terrell's upbringing played a big part in his actions during our marriage. Although he could have worked through his issues, he chose not to. Terrell adored Javeon. There was no doubt in my mind. He loved his son. He just didn't express it like most loving fathers do because he didn't know how. No one had ever taught him. No one had shown him what it meant to be a man, to be a father. The streets taught Terrell his version of manhood! Terrell didn't meet his biological father until long after we were married. Even after finding him and learning who he was, I don't think they kept in touch. I'm sure that caused even more hurt. I am not making excuses for him because you can learn anything you choose to become a better version of yourself for you and those you love. Terrell had strong men around him at church. Those men loved him, and they had his back. They would have mentored him and helped him become the man we all could see was hiding inside of him. But Terrell stayed the same and did not seek or receive the help that was in his face.

Unfortunately, Terrell didn't seem to think what he was doing was wrong. I had a lot of problems with the way Terrell handled things, including the way he handled me, the way he handled our marriage, and the way he handled himself. I was the only one who could decide if I would stay or leave. I held all the cards! I was the only one keeping myself in the marriage, and Terrell was the only one who could change himself.

Terrell and I had come from broken and dysfunctional homes. Neither of us had seen an example of a healthy marriage in our upbringing. We entered our marriage broken and unsure of how to have a successful marriage.

I expected Terrell to be my husband and my healer. Although he could have been a better husband, he could not be my healer. I had wounds from my childhood that emerged once I was in the marriage. Ones I didn't realize I had. I was raised by a single mom, and my dad wasn't active in my life. My family dynamics caused me to have attachment issues. I believed everybody who came into my life would stay. Now, I know that is so far from the truth. I expected Terrell to cling to me just as much as I clung to him because of my attachment issues. I discovered I was expecting him to do things he was incapable of doing.

I learned a marriage is where two whole people, 100% complete in themselves, come together to build, grow and share. Some say that marriage is 50/50. Well, I beg to differ. It should be 100/100. Two half people don't make a whole, complete marriage. Two half people make a disastrous marriage. I needed to be healed before getting married. We both needed to work on ourselves and be whole and complete in ourselves before entering a marriage.

Our marriage speaks of the importance of being whole, healthy, and complete in yourself because no person can complete you. Only Jesus Christ can do that. *"But let patience have its perfect work, that you may be perfect and complete, lacking nothing"*. James 1:4 (NKJV).

I deserved better, for sure. I dealt with the verbal abuse. It is an entirely different story when my child is involved. I remember thinking "you can run me through the mud, but you can't run my child through the mud." Javeon belonged to both of us, but as his mother, I felt that it was my responsibility to take care of Javeon.

As the saying goes, ain't nothing like a woman scorned. I was far beyond scorned. I had been disrespected in the worst way. I had been ignored. I had been treated like a stranger in the street. I had to deal with the mountains of insecurities piled on top of even more insecurities I carried daily. I felt worthless. I felt like giving up. BUT God showed up and blessed me with a bundle of joy, someone to help me find my way back to Him. He blessed me to be somebody's mother. I had to be tough even when I didn't feel like it or didn't feel like I could be! I had a life that I was responsible for.

That was a total game changer for me. I barely cared about my own life, but Javeon's life mattered. Javeon was going to live better and be better than me. Power and strength came from within me that I never, ever knew existed. As I think about everything I went through, I see now God used motherhood to save my life. God knew exactly what I needed and when to send him into my life. If it had not been for Javeon, I would have continued down a horrible path that would have been hard to come back from.

Though I never even wanted children, I found purpose the moment I heard the words "you're pregnant." I am so glad God doesn't follow our plans. Instead, He brings us to His plans for our lives. His ways are far better! I fell in love immediately upon holding Javeon for the first time and seeing his big, beautiful eyes. Now, I can't imagine life without my son.

So many changes take place when you become a mother. Strength comes from way down deep when it comes to taking care of your children. I have often heard people talk about a mother's instinct and mother's intuition, and it is the total truth. It kicks in instantly and it keeps intensifying.

Why did it take me seven years to leave… to find my voice… to stand up for myself? FEAR! I was afraid of the outcome. I was afraid of his reaction and subsequent actions.

I had to remember God is my protector and my comforter. I had to trust He would protect me during my transition. Was I was doing the right thing? I knew I had to do what was best for Javeon, my voice of reason. I often wondered if I would have had the fortitude to leave the marriage if God hadn't sent Javeon into my life.

I knew that when I let go of the marriage; I had to let go completely. I couldn't hold on to bits and pieces because it would still control my life. I had to put my needs first for the first time in my life. Self-love matters, and no, it ain't selfish! I can't give anything to anyone I haven't first given to myself.

Proceeding with the divorce wasn't an easy decision, considering Terrell's illness. I wanted to make sure I wasn't proceeding with the divorce during his illness just to get even or to make him feel the hurt he had caused me over the previous years. Was my decisions coming from a healthy place? I prayed and sought God for clarity and assurance. God assured me continuing with the divorce was not out of ill will. It was simply how this part of the story would end. One of Terrell's favorite scriptures was Ezekiel 11:19 (NKJV). "*Then I will give them one heart, and I will put a new spirit within them, and take the stony heart out of their flesh, and give them a heart of flesh.*" This scripture spoke to me. I asked God if I was operating from a heart of stone or a heart of flesh as I continued with the divorce.

God would remind me Terrell created his story. In the same way, I created my story. He wrote the pages that led him to facing a divorce while I made choices and wrote the pages that led me to filing for divorce. Everything always comes full circle. Knowing I would have to bear the responsibility of keeping up a household and being a single mom was unsettling as well. However, I had been doing the bulk of everything myself, anyway! We would be just fine. We had God on our side.

Life deals us all different situations and scenarios, some more devastating than others. One thing is for sure… There is nothing new under the sun. Someone else had been through what I was going through. Sometimes, just hearing of how God helped someone overcome a situation like mine was all the encouragement I needed. God's word was definitely my guide to help me navigate my life. He needed me to learn how to be reachable and relatable to show others they too are built to overcome.

During the year that Terrell and I were separated, I discovered a new version of myself. I learned how to live and not merely exist. My Voice of Reason had to be born at the time he was born. Because of his birth, I now live! May 5, 2007, is the day my new life began. I am a living testimony that God is the God of another chance. He never stopped forgiving me. He never stopped correcting me. He never took away my opportunities to get it right again. Even when I stopped listening to Him and made decisions that took me out of His perfect will and planted me firmly into His permissive will. Thank you, Jesus, for continuing to give me as many do-overs as it takes to head in the right direction in life.

My soul was happy, and it hadn't been for a very long time. I was in a place of peace and serenity. I was in a place where God had brought me. I could feel the happiness oozing from my soul. I was in my rightful place. My soul was smiling. I was feeling the new me! I had overcome! I had overcome the things that could have easily broken me or caused me to take my life. With God's strength, I survived the very thing that the enemy designed to kill me!

The things I have overcome are now pieces of my story, pieces of my testimony! This is My Story, My Testimony, and My Legacy! I am Built to

Overcome! Thank you, Jesus!!! I didn't think I had the strength to fight. God has shown me what He's put within me. I made it, and you can too! I am Built to Overcome, and so are you! *"Beloved, I pray that you may prosper in all things and be in health, just as your soul prospers."* III John 1:2 (NKJV) God was breathing this scripture into me. I was inhaling and exhaling this scripture with every breath I took!

For once, I was learning it was right to love others, but I shouldn't lose myself in the process. I could feel a new boldness emerging within me. A new Pam was on the horizon. I did not know what God was about to do through me. I had no idea how much He was about to grow me up into who He created me to be. This was about to become one beautiful journey. I was imperfectly perfect, beautifully broken, and fabulously flawed, and because of Jesus, I am still here to share my wisdom with you on the pages of this book!

My Voice of Reason made it all worth it. Terrell and I had our problems. But if I didn't meet Terrell, I wouldn't have my Javeon! Javeon makes me and the world better with his presence. Having him gave me a greater appreciation for my mother and caused me to seek God for an intimate relationship with Him.

God allowed me to lose myself to find the new version hanging out just beneath the surface. God did a new thing in me. I am a new creation. God allowed me to go through circumstances that only He could help me get through. And He gets all the praise and all the glory for my victory.

"Behold, I will do a new thing, now it shall spring forth; Shall you not know it? I will even make a road in the wilderness and rivers in the desert." Isaiah 43:19. (NKJV)

For My Good

My best friend, Shelly, and I met in middle school. By our freshman year of high school, we were inseparable. We were only a year apart, and we had a lot in common! We got our first job together and went to the same salon to get our hair done by the same stylist. We hung out at the same places after school. Shelly would even walk to my bus stop each day so we could ride to school together. There was no me without her!

Our high school graduation was particularly memorable. After I had crossed the stage to get my diploma, I immediately looked for Shelly. I could vaguely hear her calling my name, but I couldn't see her through the crowd of graduates. When we finally spotted each other, we pushed through the crowd and made it to one another. We embraced each other with the biggest and longest hug that we'd ever given one another. We were so proud we had graduated. We were happy we could share that moment and so many other experiences together.

Shelly and I remained best friends after high school. We talked daily, double dated, shopped together, traveled together, and more. As time went on, we learned to value and appreciate true friendship. When different situations arose in our lives, we always knew we could turn to one another. It was a fantastic relationship all the way around.

Shelly remained my best friend into adulthood. I was the matron of honor in her wedding, and she was my matron of honor as well. We were each there for the births of one another's children. I was honored to be the godmother of her children, and she became Javeon's godmother. After we finished college, we even ventured into entrepreneurship together. Shelly took the leap first. I joined in soon after. Our lives were intricately woven together. We really were two peas in a pod.

Of course, we shared all the details about the guys we dated over the years. We had been on some terrible double dates. And we had both been in some terrible relationships. During her dating years, there seemed to be one guy that kept Shelly on an emotional roller coaster ride for a couple of years. Bobby was a peculiar character. He would do these disappearing acts while he was dating Shelly. Then he would pop up again as if nothing happened. Bobby's behavior was far from normal. After a couple of years of this on again and off again relationship, Shelly became fed up with his behavior. She ended the relationship.

Finding decent men during our young adult years seemed to be impossible, but we never gave up hope on finding true love. Eventually, Shelly and I both married. Sadly, we would have to witness and support each other through our marriages and eventual divorces.

After I divorced Terrell, I was single for a few years. I was determined that I would use this time to strengthen my relationship with God. I was committed to finding my identity by drawing closer to God. I wanted an intimate relationship with God and with myself. This time, I wanted to do things the right way. I wanted God to send me His absolute best. That meant I had to give Him my absolute best. I made a promise to God I would keep my temple holy and set apart for my husband, the man He had chosen for me. I vowed to be celibate until my true love found me.

It wasn't long before the temptation came. I went on a few dates. I attempted to make each Mr. Wrong my Mr. Right. My loneliness made me vulnerable. One day, I received an inbox message from Bobby. What did my best friend's ex want from me? My curiosity got the best of me. I clicked on the message to read it.

The message said everything that I needed and wanted to hear. His words stopped me in my tracks and put a big smile on my face. I was eating up every letter of every word that he typed. I seemed to drift off into la la land. I was having a fairytale moment, and it felt good. We sent messages back and forth daily. Bobby seemed to know exactly what to say to make my heart melt. I had been longing to hear everything he said. I hung on every word.

During one of our conversations, Bobby said God had told him I was going to be his wife. I was shocked! I knew I would be married again. God had already promised me that. Was he the one? Was I to believe God would send my best friend's ex to be my husband? My heart was in the driver's seat as I entertained the thought, but my mind was far from quiet!

My next thought was, "You need to tell Shelly." I was reluctant and scared. I knew it was something I had to do. I had to come clean with Shelly. She was someone I had known for a huge part of my life. I loved and respected her as a person. More importantly, she was my best friend.

Shelly deserved to know what was going on between her best friend and her ex. I wasn't sure what to expect. How would she react? Would she yell, scream, curse, fuss, or fight?

I sent Shelly a text message, telling her I had something to tell her. I asked if we could meet. This conversation had to be face to face. I wasn't going to tell her any other way. I needed to see her reaction and read her emotions as I told her I was pursuing a relationship with her ex. I wanted her honest feedback. I hoped she would leave her thoughts and concerns on the table.

Shelly agreed to come to my house. When she arrived, we did our catching up and our girl talk as we always had each time we met. Then I told her. I can't even describe how I was feeling as I anticipated her reaction. I revealed I had been talking to Bobby for a couple of weeks. I admitted I was thinking about seeing where things would go with him. I told her I wanted her honest feedback about the situation. Then I held my breath and waited for her response.

Shelly didn't really seem surprised. She was actually calmer than I thought she would have been. She said she didn't think Bobby was my husband.

She reminded me of who he was when she dated him. I told her I definitely remembered how he acted during their relationship. But I also mentioned people can change. She agreed people do change, but she wasn't convinced Bobby had changed. However, she said if I wanted to see where things would go in this relationship with Bobby, then I should go for it and see where it goes. I told her I respected her for being calm, and I thanked her for her input.

I felt good about our conversation. I was glad I had her best wishes to see where things would go with Bobby. And I was grateful we were still going to be friends through all of this. In fact, it shocked me when our friendship seemed to remain the same. She never, ever seemed upset. She didn't change her actions towards me at all. It was as if I was just dating a guy, not dating her ex.

Before long, I referred to my relationship with Bobby as an online relationship. Sadly, most of our conversations were through social media. We would communicate primarily through a messaging app. I rarely heard his voice. And I hardly ever saw him. I was starting to think he was seeing someone else because we had never met in public.

Once, Bobby asked me to meet him at the park, one of my favorite places. This time, he really poured it on thickly. He captivated my mind and heart as we walked, talked, and held hands. I started imagining the great things that were to come in our relationship and our future. I was back in la la land.

After we left the park, he told me he would call me soon. That call never came. In fact, the disappearing acts began soon after. Yes, you guessed it. Bobby did the same disappearing acts that occurred when he and Shelly were dating. Nothing had changed!

When Shelly asked me how things were going with Bobby, I had to admit Bobby had been disappearing and then reappearing as if he had never left. She reminded me of how he had done the same thing with her. However, she wouldn't say anything negative about the fact I was dating her ex. She would give me her opinion as if we were talking about any other man I was dating. She seemed to handle everything well.

I was questioning my "relationship" with Bobby. Was it even a real relationship? I had only seen him face-to-face three times. And I had only spoken to him on the phone once or twice. That's some relationship, right?

What was I doing? I had told God on several occasions I was done with Bobby. He was obviously playing games. He wasn't serious about a relationship with me. Why couldn't I let go?

Believe it or not, my relationship with God was blossoming like never before, even during my "relationship" with Bobby and other mishaps. I had been selected to help with the women's ministry at church. I was going to meetings and preparing for an upcoming conference with our church ministry leaders. I was fairly new to the ministry, so I was excited about being a part of the women's ministry team.

One night, our Bible study teacher was Minister Parcell. I admired her teachings and her love for God. I adored her powerful hugs. They made me feel like I was being embraced by Jesus Himself. That night's message was about God's love. Minister Parcell was teaching about how God loves us so much. She said God goes out of His way to take care of us and to give us the desires of our heart. He gives us His absolute best!

This teaching was told through the story of an army man who was supposed to take his wife out on a date. Because of work, he was going to miss the date. Yet he still made sure his wife had a perfect evening. He bought her a beautiful gown and laid it on the bed for her. He arranged for a limo to escort her to one of her favorite restaurants. He made sure she had her favorite server and her favorite entrée. The husband ensured she would have the best night possible.

I felt as if God was speaking to my heart through Minister Parcell's message. She related this story to how God ensures we always receive His best. As I listened, I knew this was God's way of showing me I needed to end my relationship with Bobby. I pulled out a pen and began to write.

As Minister Parcell continued with her message, I was writing my "Dear John" letter to Bobby. As she spoke, I poured out my feelings onto paper. I wrote of all the wrongs I had allowed to happen over the past three months. I was fed up. The letter wasn't mean and nasty. It was just my resolve to know the relationship wasn't meant to be.

I had been carrying around dead weight for three months. I should have never allowed Bobby into my life. As I wrote the letter, I could feel a burden lifting. I could feel the shackles being released; I could feel the bondage being broken. It felt like freedom! "Yes," I remember thinking, "this is what freedom feels like!"

As Bible study ended, I packed the letter along with all my things. I was walking on clouds as I left church that night. The weight had been lifted. I felt whole and healed. I was free. I knew there would be no going back. There was such a sweet peace as I released the relationship and walked into freedom.

After I finished the letter, I went back and forth about mailing it. Was writing the letter just a way to release my feelings and emotions? I wasn't sure if I was supposed to actually mail it. Maybe it was just part of the process of me being completely and totally free from that so-called relationship. Was writing the letter God's way of helping me to dissolve the relationship with Bobby? Deep down, I wanted Bobby to understand why he was being blocked from my life. I talked to God about it in the days to come. I realized He wanted me to mail the letter. I knew Bobby's address, so I happily mailed the letter.

A few days went by, and I wondered if Bobby had received my letter. One day, I was going through the mail that I had taken from my mailbox. There it was, among the bills and junk mail. I had received the letter back. It was marked as UNDELIVERABLE. But the address was correct. I had checked and double checked it before I mailed it. I was perplexed.

Why did God have me to write the letter if Bobby would not read it? I sought God for clarity. He helped me understand the purpose of writing the letter. He showed me that the letter wasn't for Bobby. It was for me.

The letter was for my reflection and confirmation. It was an acknowledgement of my worth and the reminder I needed to remember who I am.

Meanwhile, things seemed to be going well with Shelly. She had introduced me to a business she had joined. It didn't take much for her to convince me to jump onboard. We were making strides towards building our businesses. That was our main goal. I was talking to her almost daily and seeing her a few times a week for meetings and training.

I was enjoying the business building aspect, but I was also discovering this business wasn't my passion. I wasn't getting enough clients to grow my business and sustain my household. I was becoming frustrated with myself, God, and the business. Was entrepreneurship even for me? While at one of our training sessions, I started talking to Shelly about the business God was revealing to me. I told her I was ready to quit my full-time job to follow my entrepreneurship dream.

I prayed, prayed, and prayed some more. I had to be certain this was a God thing, not just a Pam thing. By this time, I was responsible for taking care of my son and my mother. My decision would affect them as well. I had to make sure leaving corporate America was God's plan for me. If it was His plan, I knew He would cover and keep us through this journey.

I talked to my Pastor and shared my thoughts with him as well. I explained how I planned to maintain my household as I continued to grow my business. My Pastor has a background in finance and entrepreneurship. I knew if I had his approval and God's, then it was a go. I got a thumbs up from him, so that was the icing on the cake that I needed.

The day came for me to turn in my resignation. I had been at this job for 12 years, but I knew this was the right move. I fired corporate America! Guess who was right there with me? Shelly! I don't know which one of us was more excited.

After letting go of Bobby, I seemed to walk in my purpose even more. The pieces of my life puzzle seemed to come together. For a long time, I was clueless as to God's purposes for me. It was becoming clearer to me.

I was birthing another business. I had also created a women's networking event. I was so glad I had decided to walk in obedience. I was grateful for God's guidance, grace, and mercy. Every day I was learning more about Him and myself.

Things were coming along smoothly as I worked towards getting my new business off the ground, but I was noticing some changes with Shelly. She seemed distant. I didn't talk to her as often. Since I had fired corporate America, I had more time to hang out with her. When I would ask if she wanted to meet, she always had something else to do.

Meanwhile, my interest in the business I had joined with Shelly was fading. She was happy about my new business, but she also wanted me to be devoted to the business I had joined with her. I was feeling like something had to give. I was going to have to let go of the business I shared with Shelly. Besides, I needed to focus on building my business. I got around to telling Shelly I would not continue in the business with her anymore. She wasn't pleased with the news. She told me she didn't think my work with that company was done. I knew it was time for me to go in a different direction. I found my peace with God on the issue.

There were so many things going on in my life, yet it seemed more and more difficult to share my moments with Shelly. It saddened me when I reflected on what was quickly becoming distant memories, when our phone calls would normally last for hours. In the past, we had so much to share with one another. Those moments were dissipating. It didn't feel good. It hurt. My lifelong friendship seemed to be fading.

I continued to reach out to Shelly. I would ask if we could meet and talk, yet I would get excuse after excuse. Finally, she agreed to meet with me. I was anticipating our meeting. I had missed her so much. When that day came, I couldn't have braced myself for what I heard her say. "I know things have been different," she said, stating the obvious. The flood gates opened from there. Shelly told me she had been attending meetings with some other female friends over the last few months. "Okay," I thought. Shelly was having conversations and prayers with these ladies. During one meeting, the lady told her someone was stabbing her in the back, someone close to her. "No way," I thought. I listened, honestly bewildered. Then Shelly dropped the bomb on me. The backstabber was supposedly me! I think I stopped breathing for a few seconds. Me? I'm the backstabber? I couldn't be hearing this right!

Shelly said God was placing women in her life, and she was growing really close to them. They were growing great relationships. I took that as if she were saying God had already sent her my replacement. The dagger seemed to go deeper into my heart. Wait, hold on a second! What is happening right now?

I wasn't ready for anything I heard Shelly say. I was stunned. I cried like a woman who was losing her best friend of 25 years. That's exactly what was happening! Shelly said a lot to me in a very short amount of time. In my astonishment, I had caught the gist of it all.

After Shelly left, I didn't know how to feel. I was numb. How did we get here? How did this happen? Did this really just happen? Am I dreaming? Was I waking up from a nightmare?

I pulled myself together and made my way to my car. I thought about her words. Was this about Bobby? Was she angry because I had left the business? Was I a backstabber? I may be a lot of things, but I had never been called a backstabber! Plus, she would be the last one I would stab! How could two people who had shared everything with one another for 25 years suddenly no longer be friends? Shelly had been a part of my life for so long, I couldn't imagine my life without her. What was my life going to look like from this point? How could I move on from here?

Months passed before I talked to Shelly again. Then one day, she called me. I was hesitant to answer when I saw her name as my phone rang. A bigger part of me wanted to hear her voice. I was curious to hear what she had to say.

Shelly had called to apologize for the words she used that day. She apologized for hurting me. I told her I had taken responsibility for my part in everything. I forgave her for everything that had happened between us. I also told her I didn't know what the future held for us. I didn't know if we would ever be friends again. If so, I doubted our friendship would ever be the same. There was no way of going back to what was after hearing the things she had said to me. I hated our close friendship had to end, especially how it did.

The distance between Shelly and me grew steadily. Occasionally, Shelly would post something on social media. It was my only glimpse at what was going on in her life. We would also have brief chats via text from time to time. And I would send celebratory messages on her children's birthdays, as well as on hers.

A couple of years would pass before I saw Shelly again. It surprised me to see her at one of my women's networking events. We took pictures together. She applauded the success of my business. For a second, it almost felt like the good ol' days. I reminisced for a moment. But after the event, the distance between us remained.

A Deeper Look…

It is definitely true, before Mr. Right shows up a bunch of Mr. Wrongs try their best to capture your attention. Never in a million years would I think one of the Mr. Wrongs would be my best friend's ex. How did I fall for that?

Bobby was a slickster. He played that same game he had played with Shelly for years. I was weak, so I fell for it. He tapped into my vulnerabilities! He knew what I needed and so desperately wanted –to be loved. I became his puppet. He was pulling my strings and toying with my emotions. This situation had betrayal written all over it, and I missed all the warning signs.

I had tried to make myself feel better about the situation. "We don't get to choose who we fall in love with," I told myself. Wait. What? I seriously couldn't have been in love with a man who had only sent me text messages! I was blinded by what could be. I was enticed by the mirage of the love I so desperately wanted. But I was in the wrong place, at the wrong time, with the wrong person.

Although Shelly never admitted it, I knew our problems began when my relationship with Bobby began. I wish Shelly had honestly shared her feelings with me. Perhaps this could have changed my course of actions. It doesn't always feel good, but sometimes we need to have those uneasy conversations. The lines of communication must remain open for our relationships to remain healthy. When Shelly stopped openly and honestly sharing her feelings with me, our relationship began to die.

In hindsight, I can clearly see I was wrong. The girl code was broken. Shelly wasn't just a girl I knew, a mere acquaintance. She was my dearest, closest friend. How could I? Not once did I ever think I could do anything to sabotage our relationship or cause it to end so abruptly and in such a hurtful way.

I take full responsibility for what I did. We can't go back and change what happened. I wish I could! How, or better yet, why, did I allow a three-month long fantasy to destroy a friendship that took 25 years to build? I'm thankful Bobby and I didn't have sex during those three months. So why did he have such a hold on me? I kept asking myself, "How did I allow this to happen?"

Desperation! It was a snare of the enemy. But it was also a divine setup from God. This situation reminded me of a sermon called "He set me up just to bless me." That's exactly what God was doing in my life.

By the time I met Bobby, I had been battling negative self-esteem for years. Bobby's words played into my weakness and lack of self-esteem. It's amazing how his words impacted me, even though I didn't hear them. Bobby's text messages and brief encounters seeped into my spirit. I didn't know to ask God to teach me how to protect my eye and ear gates against the plot of the enemy. God was showing me how what I read and hear can seep into my spirit. Regardless of how we receive them, WORDs have power!

After my divorce, God promised another man would never hurt me. I had lost sight of God's promise during those months with Bobby. In hindsight, I can clearly see the relationship would not end well for me, but I was still holding on to what could be. God would give me signs Bobby wasn't who He had for me. He began to show me how I was allowing my self-esteem issues to cloud my judgement and showed me I needed to be healed in that area. I couldn't stand firmly on His promises if I was still entertaining Bobby's foolishness.

Even though I was partly disgusted with myself, part of me was accepting of the mess that I was calling a relationship. I was embracing the counterfeit love that Bobby portrayed. Bobby said God had told him that I would be his wife. Then he would disappear for weeks at a time. Clearly, we were not having the same conversations with the same God! Why was I so confused about this entire situation?

I had fallen into the enemy's trap, with every strategically placed stinking word! The enemy tried to distract me and keep me from what God had promised me. It was ALL meant to steal, kill, and destroy my destiny. But God!!! He turned that situation around and used it for my good.

My "relationship" with Bobby went back and forth until God became fed up with my foolishness. I am so glad that He loves us unconditionally, and He will never give up on us. He is the God of a second, third, fourth, and fifth chance. The purpose, the gifts, and the love that He places within us can't be wasted. He is fully invested in His prized possessions. He will never leave us nor forsake us!

The lessons I learned from that one situation have enriched my life in ways I cannot begin to express. I don't have the words to explain how God continued talking and pouring into me, even when I wasn't listening. God was working behind the scenes to turn that negative into a positive. The crazy thing about the whole situation was the more attached I became to Bobby, the more I heard God's voice. It amazes every time I think about how God allowed Proverbs 16:9 (NKJV) to play out in my life. "*A man's heart plans his way, but the Lord directs his steps.*"

God used this situation to show me who I am in Him once again. I had to allow Him to show me what LOVE really is. I couldn't continue to play the what if game or even the would of, could of, and/or should of game to excuse the part I played in the situation. The truth of the matter is, if I had put my trust in God, it would not have needed to happen. It had to happen to redirect me to the path God ordained for me to travel.

God is a promise keeper, and He is very intentional. He keeps His word. He is strategic. He takes care of His own. He is truly amazing! God knows our heart, and He knows when we have totally released a situation to Him. God knew that if I continued in that fake relationship, it would take me further into negative self-esteem. As always, He stepped in right in the nick of time.

I was holding on for dear life to this false relationship. I was acting as if Bobby was the only man who would ever take an interest in me. I was acting hopeless. With God, I should always be hopeful. Although God had been helping me with my self-esteem issues for the past few years, it was obvious that I had forgotten my worth and my value.

I knew what God had promised me, and I thought I was ready for my one true husband and leave my past behind me. But I still had work to do to freely embrace who God says I am. I needed to surrender my deepest fear and my heart's desire before I could receive what God promised.

I still had places inside my heart that needed to be healed. I needed to be made whole. And I was ok with that! Especially on those occasions when my attitude kept me stuck in situations longer than necessary. It sounds crazy, but Bobby helped me to regain my self-esteem once and for all. Even though this chapter in my life wasn't great, it helped me get my life in order.

Before Bobby came along, I had promised myself I was going to draw closer to God while I was single. At the first hint of some attention from a man, I forgot everything I said. But God didn't! He reminded me I am wondrously and fearfully made in His image! (Psalm 139:14 NKJV) I am forever grateful to God for not allowing me to compromise, settle, and/or forfeit all the growth I had achieved. He saw my worth and my value, even when I didn't. Now, I have a message to share with the world of how God showed me glimpses of who He made me to be and tuned my spiritual ears to hear Him clearly.

God had to heal my hurt before I could go deeper into my purpose. Earlier, I shared how I believe everything happens for a reason. This journey showed me how God turned my pain into purpose when I surrendered. Some days I wanted to quit, and wallow in the hurt, pain, and shame of my past. But God! He came to my rescue and put me back on the path that leads to restoration and healing.

God was standing at the door, knocking. I had to open the door to my heart and let Him in. He was working it out in my favor and for my good! *"And we know that in all things God works for the good of those who love Him, who have been called according to His purpose."* Romans 8:28 NIV

Timeless

The night I decided to let go of that so-called relationship with Bobby, I instantly felt freedom. God had set me free from the negative self-esteem. My God reminded me of my worth. As I left Bible study that night, I valued myself more, and I loved myself more.

I would usually spend time catching up with my sister and other church members after Bible study. We would talk so long that we would get put out of the church. We would always end up in the church parking lot to talk some more. This night was no exception. As we talked, I shared what God had revealed to me during Bible study.

Other members were exiting the church and walking towards the parking lot as well. As I was talking to my sister, I noticed someone walking in our direction. I knew he was a male by the way he walked. The swag was real, but I couldn't really see him. As he came into my view, my eyes basked in the beauty that was him. He was gorgeous!

I watched him as he walked to his car. There was something about him. His swag was different. Everything about him was different. I was so focused on him I completely forgot what I was saying. I didn't realize I had stopped talking mid-sentence and began talking about the handsome man walking towards us. The look on their faces was priceless! As he approached his car, I got a better look at him. My confidence kicked in and I found the courage to speak. "Hey, how are you doing?" I asked. I think he replied, "I'm good" or "How are you?" I couldn't even focus on his response. All I knew was that he responded to my greeting. My Lord! Who is this man? How had I missed him?

On the same night I surrendered everything to God, this happens! On the night I let go of the baggage, God said "It is Finished." Then I see this man who stopped me in my tracks. I know I still have work to do on me. Did God allow me to experience my recent set back to set me up for a blessing? Now, I'm really feeling like this night couldn't get any better!

After I spoke to him in the parking lot that night, I didn't talk to him again until a few weeks later. I found out his name is Elvin, and I made it my business to spot him in church every Sunday morning. I couldn't take my eyes off him.

A couple weeks went by, and I finally got a social media friend request from him. Yes! I happily accepted that Facebook request. About a week later, I noticed he messaged me through the app. Oh, happy day! I was at my daddy's house when I got the message. I did my happy dance. The look on daddy's face was priceless. Daddy looked at my sister and asked, "What is wrong with her? What just happened?" No one knew I had been anxiously awaiting this message. I told my sister the guy from church had sent me a message. Poor daddy he was looking totally confused. Social media was foreign to him. I said, "I'm dancing because a guy from church just sent me a message." "What?" he said loudly, like only he can! It was hilarious!

After a few days of chatting through messenger, he sent me a message and said, "I'm old school. All this messaging ain't for me." I could tell through his messages he had a sense of humor. He said, "Here's my number. Call me so you won't think I'm stalking you!" Now, why would I think such a thing?

We talked daily. It was great getting to know him. It was even better to have someone pursuing me. When he said he was going to call, he would. Our conversations were fun and just what I needed. I loved the little game we played each day. We would each ask the other person our question of the day. The question of the day could be about something current, something from our past, or something we looked forward to happening in the future. One of his most memorable questions to me was "What is your perfect Saturday?" Elvin asked me to walk him through what would happen on my perfect Saturday. What would I do from the time I woke until I went to bed? Where would I go? What would I eat? Who would I want to see? What would I want to do? He wanted to know every detail.

Until that point, no one had ever piqued my interest the way he did. Elvin made me think about life and what I wanted out of life. He made me dig deeper and think about my future. Elvin differed from all the other guys I had known. I enjoyed everything about him. I looked forward to getting to know more about him.

We continued talking daily for about a month before Elvin asked me out. We kept our relationship private, especially from the people at church. This was new for the both of us, and we wanted to get to know one another before revealing our news. Although we were low key, I would purposely make my way to him in church during fellowship time to get one of his good old "secret" hugs.

Elvin called me one Sunday after leaving a meeting at church. He asked if we could meet. Oh, yeah! I was finally going to see him other than at church. Now we were about to see if the relationship would grow or fizzle. If we liked each other in person as much as we liked each other on the phone, we most definitely would move forward.

We met at a popular restaurant that was convenient for the both of us. I was out with my family when he called. I quickly left them to go meet him. My sister knew how exciting this was for me, so she covered for me.

By the time I arrived at the restaurant, Elvin was already seated. When I walked through the door, I immediately saw him. I had a terrible case of the butterflies from the excitement of seeing him. The butterflies kicked into over-drive the moment I sat down. We started talking and the butterflies slowly went away. We both were getting involved with different ministries at church, and we started talking about the ministries. Elvin had been asked to be a part of the men's ministry committee. That intrigued me because the ministry leader had asked me to be on our women's ministry committee. It seemed as if everything was falling into place as it relates to our growth in God. We talked about his meeting with the men's ministry, our children and families. There was no subject off limits. The more we talked and ate, the more relaxed I became.

Elvin was easy to talk to. I'm usually nervous when I first meet someone, but not this time! I'm sure we were there for about two and a half hours. The conversation was just as great in person as it had been over the phone. When we left the restaurant, he walked me to my car. We chatted a bit more. Then he gave me the infamous "church hug." I had enjoyed everything about our date. The results were in... we liked each other in person, too!

Our relationship progressed over the next few weeks. We were really getting to know one another, and I was enjoying every second. I was loving everything I learned about him. His honesty meant everything to me. The sincerity was there, and it was real. It just felt right! We both seemed to know what we wanted in a relationship. It was perfectly clear we had to be honest with one another for things to continue to grow between us.

After our first date, we started meeting after Bible Study. I enjoyed his company. Elvin seemed to be cut from a different cloth. He intrigued me. I respected his honesty, and I adored our conversations. He actually pursued me! He cared for me in a way I had never experienced. His genuineness was refreshing. I felt like I could trust him with my heart, and it wouldn't be shattered into a million tiny pieces. His words always lined up with his actions. I was digging him on every level.

As the days went by, Elvin and I talked several times a day! I always looked forward to talking to him and seeing him even more. Everything seemed to fall into place. We were dating for a few months before we started talking about making our relationship official. I think we both knew this relationship was going somewhere, and it would blossom into more than a friendship.

Things were going so great, too great. I started thinking that he might do or say the wrong thing. I was praying and hoping he never would. Those were my thoughts from time to time. Things between us seemed perfect, and I was loving it. I was beyond thrilled about the beginnings of my very own love story. I love everything about love. I love relationship building, engagements, marriages, and everything romantic. Elvin was sweeping me off my feet and I loved every moment of it.

The little things became big things to him. I remember when Elvin asked me to meet him at a car wash, so he could clean my headlight covers and give Maxine (my car) a good cleaning. I couldn't believe it. I hadn't ever thought about asking anyone to clean my headlight covers. That he noticed this little thing blew my mind. He worked wonders. I barely recognized Maxine when he was done. At that moment, I realized how much my relationship with Elvin meant to me. He was a man of his word. If he said he was going to do something, he did it. That was a big deal for me.

Our conversations were non-stop from that point forward. We didn't have any silence while we were talking. It seemed as if we always had something to talk about. I loved that about him. He was an excellent communicator, and I needed that in my life. I was drawn in with his every word. Elvin unknowingly offered some much-needed balance in my life. He would not let me fall back into the quiet and shy aspect of my personality. He helped me to open up more than I ever imagined I could.

Two months into our relationship, we made plans to meet downtown. It was one of my favorite local places. We walked, talked, and held hands. Elvin knew I loved taking pictures, so I became his model for the day. We did a mini photo shoot, and I loved every second of it. I was scared to walk across the bridge because I don't like heights over water. But being held by Elvin made it just a tad bit easier for me.

I loved spending the day with Elvin. We walked and talked. Then we walked and talked some more until he had to leave for work. We were parked in different areas, so Elvin walked me to my car. He was always a total gentleman. That day, I reached into my car and pulled out a surprise.

It was our two-month anniversary, so I had to do something a little extra. Surprise! I held up the gift bag to show him and handed it to him. He wasn't expecting that to happen. He had a very appealing smirk on his face. His smile melted my heart every time. "What's this?", he asked. "It's our anniversary today, so I had to get you something," I said. As he opened the bag, I happily watched him check out his gift. The greeting card and the gift bag had the same scripture, even though I hadn't planned it that way. *"Though one may be overpowered by another, two can withstand him. And a threefold cord is not easily broken."* (Ecclesiastes 4:12 NKJV) I hoped we were building that type of foundation for our relationship.

We would talk and laugh about when we wanted to "officially" reveal that we were dating. I was so in love and our relationship was blossoming beautifully. I would tease him by saying I would save a seat for him beside me at church. He would laugh and say, "I'm not ready yet." Elvin would kid around and say I was going to have to move from my seat and come to the back of the church with him. I had already decided he was going to move closer to the front with me. "Come and get closer to the fire," I told him.

We had been seeing one another about three months when our pastor decided to have a church anniversary dinner. We decided to do our big reveal at the dinner. I was so excited! I couldn't wait! That evening, I arrived at the church dinner before Elvin. I had already gotten food for my mother and Javeon. I was standing in line to fix my plate when I saw him come in. I waved at him to come and stand with me. He did not want to do that. I didn't think about the fact he would be cutting the line. Bless my heart! Eventually, we both got our food, and Elvin came and sat with me. I was so excited! I also had a case of the nerves.

Our relationship wasn't new to us, but it was new to our church family. I think we had done a good job of keeping our relationship quiet. It wasn't top secret news, but we wanted to wait and see where things were going first. Now, we were both willing to let the outside world know about our newly brewing relationship.

Our news was out! No more secrets. Now Elvin could start sitting with me in church. I was looking forward to that. For years, I had been the one seeing husbands and boyfriends with their arms around their ladies during church, and I remember thinking, "one day it would be my turn." Well, my day was just around the corner, and I was giddy with excitement and anticipation!

Now that our relationship was out in the open, some ladies at church asked about our relationship and how it started. I would happily tell them we weren't looking for one another, but God said it was time for both of us. This was a God thing through and through!

As our relationship progressed, I would look forward to our nightly conversations. I would talk to Elvin for as long as he would permit. I remember him repeatedly saying, "I gotta go because I gotta get up in the morning for work. I'm going to be mad at you when I wake up sleepy." But our conversations were so great. We couldn't resist the opportunity to get to know one another better. It was so hard to say bye and actually hang up the phone.

One conversation that we had stands out in my memory. I still get mushy about it. It was obvious to both of us early in our relationship we had something to hold on to in each other. Even though it was early in our relationship, our feelings for each other were deep. I remember one night in particular; that night was the absolute cutest, and here's why! Before he hung up the phone with me that night, he said, "I like you a lot!" It was too early in our relationship for him to tell me he loved me. Instead, he chose to say the cutest, most memorable thing to me. I will always remember his words.

Things shifted for me at that moment. I had been thinking I was crazy for falling in love with him so quickly. Did I really love him? Was it too soon to be feeling what I was feeling? Now, I had answers to those questions. I wasn't crazy. He was feeling the same thing.

Having my feelings affirmed by Elvin felt good. However, I must admit it was a bit scary, too. Actually, I was terrified. The last time I opened my heart to someone, things didn't end well. But God told me I would never be hurt by a man again. Maybe Elvin was my true soulmate. This was really happening! Elvin had popped into my life when I didn't expect him, and he was sweeping me off my feet!

Our relationship was growing day by day. The time had come for Elvin to meet my favorite dude, Javeon. Javeon had heard me talk about Elvin many times. It was time for them to meet. On that day, Javeon was quite the gentleman, and things went well. I was so glad to have them meet. They seemed fond of one another. Everything seemed to fall into place. The icing on the cake was when Javeon gave Elvin the biggest hug ever after Bible study one night. I wasn't expecting it. Elvin wasn't, either. Later that night, Elvin and I were talking on the phone. He told me he was so surprised when Javeon hugged him. Elvin said that made his day!

A short while later, a minister from church planned a theater show and dinner event. Elvin and I were excited about going. Elvin loved the theatre and live shows. It wasn't something that interested me. I hadn't been to a live theatre show before, but I was looking forward to it. I was looking forward to dressing up and getting extra cute. I wanted to see Elvin get sharp, too. It was going to be a night to remember, no doubt!

The drive to the venue was hilarious because Elvin was nervous about us showing up together. Not all our congregation knew we were "an item." However, that was about to change. More of our church family were about to find out. I was happy about showing up with Elvin. I was ready to arrive hand-in-hand with my Mr. Wonderful.

Everything about the theatre show and dinner was excellent! Elvin truly enjoyed himself because he was in his element. The show was phenomenal, and the food was delicious! After a great show and dinner, we went to my favorite place, the waterfall. Once again, Elvin was an absolute gentleman from beginning to end. He opened my car door. We walked and held hands. He made me feel like nothing else mattered at that moment. He respected and cherished me. Something I wasn't used to receiving.

If you haven't figured it out, I am a picture fanatic. I love capturing moments and taking selfies. That night, I became his model once again. As we were walking, we came upon some purple lights by the waterfall. The pictures came out great! Not only was I extra cute, but I was with the man of my dreams at one of my favorite places. I am sure God had them to place purple lights there just for me! God favors me! That night was truly special!

On another occasion, Elvin asked me if I would like to go on a weekend trip to Atlanta. With no hesitation, I happily said yes. Elvin was quite the gentleman. I absolutely loved that Elvin put time and thought into pleasing me. Elvin initiated and planned things. He was pursuing me. I had not experienced anything like this in any of my previous relationships. I loved how things were progressing.

I remember Elvin telling my sister he was going to let me drive to Atlanta while he just chilled in the passenger's seat. When he came to pick me up on the morning of the trip, I was prepared to drive. I hate driving in Atlanta, but I figured if he was taking me on a weekend getaway, the least I could do was drive there. Besides, he said he would drive back.

Well, as I was headed to the car, Elvin made his way in front of me and opened the passenger door. Oh, my goodness! Elvin had been kidding the whole time. Thank you, Jesus! Elvin never intended for me to drive. He was planning to drive there and back. And my sister knew it all along. They were plotting behind my back!

I couldn't believe it. The man of my dreams was taking me on a weekend getaway. I was both nervous and excited yet again. We arrived in Atlanta and had the best time. We stayed in a really nice hotel downtown. This was the first time that I had experienced valet parking. This was all new to me, but I was loving every minute of it. Elvin exposed me to things I knew existed but had never experienced. He treated me like royalty.

He didn't have any expectations of me that weekend. I didn't have to worry about him crossing any boundaries. I remember waking up and just staring at him as he gazed out of the window. The skyline was beautiful, but all I could do was watch him. Although I was seeing him from behind, I could tell he was in a peaceful place and taking advantage of the opportunity to meditate. As he sipped his tea, I could only pray to God Elvin remained a part of my story. Even though it was still early in our relationship, I knew he had to be my life partner. The ease with which we talked made our quiet time that much more peaceful and special. My life was already better because he was a part of it. It could only get better going forward. I hated when our weekend came to an end, but I returned home with some great memories.

I would always look forward to seeing Elvin every chance I got. It was even better when looked forward to seeing him at church, where it all began. I knew this was God-ordained. It wasn't because we met at church, but because everything was lining up perfectly. No human could take credit for this.

Elvin and I would usually meet after Bible Study to get something to eat. Mainly, we just wanted to be together. There's nothing like spending time with the person who makes you better. We would talk about our day and make plans for the weekend. Within three to four months, we were talking about being in a committed relationship. I was head over hills in love with Elvin! Wow, had I really fallen in love with him? Was this true love? We both wanted to spend as much time together as possible. We both knew what we wanted. As we continued to learn more about one another, our feelings became more than "I like you a lot."

Falling in love with Elvin was easy to do. He was everything I needed and wanted. But I wanted to make sure I kept my promises to God first and foremost. I had been celibate since my divorce, and I wanted to remain that way. Our feelings for one another grew quickly. I think it was not only because our relationship was God-ordained, but because we just didn't see it coming. Neither one of us was looking for a relationship when we found one another. Which makes it even more amazing!

Elvin was developing a great relationship with Javeon, and you know that touched my heart. Javeon would look forward to spending time with Elvin when he would come to our house. Elvin would read Javeon bedtime stories some nights. Things were unfolding right before my eyes. Was this really my life?

We were preparing for the holiday season. Sometimes, Elvin would go home to see his family for the weekend. I was happy knowing he had a great relationship with his mother and his children. I just wasn't excited about not seeing him on those days. Yep, I was being selfish!

Because of my Mother's dementia, I became the cook for Thanksgiving. It made me hate Alzheimer's even more. My mother could throw down in the kitchen and I missed her cooking! This Thanksgiving, Elvin was going to be tasting my cooking for the first time. Even though he went home for Thanksgiving, he made it back early enough to spend that evening with me and my family. I was both nervous and excited. I was thinking about our future and the meals I would prepare for him when we were married. Especially since I had become Mrs. Pam Dorsey in his latest text messages!

We had been dating for approximately three months. Elvin came to my house one day and informed me we were officially boyfriend and girlfriend. We had put a title on it. Elvin is funny. He said he had to give me a 90-day probationary period to make sure everything lined up. Although he "likes me a lot" and sometimes refers to me as Mrs. Pam Dorsey, he still had to give it 90 days before I was "officially" his girlfriend. After he declared us official, he prayed for us. Amazing!

My Timeless Love had arrived! He was the real deal. To seal the deal, he prayed for me, and for us! When God does a thing, you know that it's from Him!

We were getting close to the Christmas holiday, and Elvin was ready for me to meet his mom. Oh, wow! I wasn't sure how I felt about it. This was big, major! When you're meeting momma, things are serious. She was coming to our city to visit some friends, so Elvin decided that would be the perfect time for me to meet her. The date was set. We had planned to meet her at a restaurant to have a Christmas luncheon.

I was nervous with anticipation. But Elvin's mom was the nicest, sweetest, and most beautiful lady I had ever met. They say that you can tell a lot about a man by the way he treats his mother. Well, Elvin really impressed me. I could tell he had a loving relationship with his mother. She gave me gifts, and she sent some gifts home with me for Javeon. She was very warm and welcoming. That meant the world to me. It's one thing to accept me, but accepting my child warms my heart. She was literally welcoming my child into her family. A few days later, Elvin and I went to his hometown to visit his mother. I had even more time to get to know her. She was so hospitable. Her home was warm and cozy. I got to see where Elvin was born and raised, in the home his dad had built from the ground up.

Elvin and I had been planning to go to a popular restaurant in Charlotte, North Carolina. I was excited about taking another road trip with my Mr. Wonderful. When we arrived, we had a 45-minute wait. In the meantime, we browsed through some stores in the mall. I already knew that I loved this man with everything within me. But this trip confirmed it all.

On that beautiful day, I knew Elvin had to be a part of my story. He had to be in my life for the rest of my days. It was the way he held me! He somehow knew exactly how I wanted and needed to be held. The way he looked into my eyes as we stood and talked left me breathless then and still leaves me breathless today. The way Elvin loved me through his touch was amazing. To me, it was something only the man that God specifically created for me would know how to do. The most romantic, breathtaking moments of my life were happening as we stood in the lobby of that restaurant. I was the center of his attention. His focus was solely on me. I felt as if I was the only person in the restaurant. Time stood still long enough for me to bask in the moment. I will never, ever forget how he made me feel in the moment. The love I saw in his eyes mesmerized me. When I looked at him, it was as if he was looking through me and into the depths of my soul. As we gazed into one another's eyes, he rubbed the small of my back, and I knew he was the one.

That night, Elvin made me feel like nothing and no one else mattered. God had sent me the man of my dreams. He was the man with whom I was destined to spend the rest of my life with. God had sent the man He created specifically for me. It was clear to me our souls had met long before our bodies ever did. God made this man just for me. He made this man with me in mind. God knew everything I would need in a man to become better and to fulfill my life's purpose. He wrapped it all up into a lovely, valuable, priceless, and tremendously handsome package. Then He placed a purple bow on it and breathed life into him. God had granted me the desires of my heart. *"Delight yourself also in the Lord, and He shall give you the desires of your heart."* Psalms 38:10 NKJV.

Over the days and weeks to come, our love intensified. We talked about how quickly things had progressed between us. We talked about getting married and what our ideal time frame would be. Elvin kept saying we could date for two years and be engaged for two years. I wasn't in agreement with that not-so-funny humor. I would tell him it doesn't take four years to determine if I'm the one for him. Four years just wasn't an option.

My suspense was growing. I would have married him that day if he had asked. Elvin would joke with me and say we wouldn't be married anytime soon. We talked about having more children. I said I wanted at least one more because I wanted a girl. Elvin has older children, so he wasn't as excited about having more children. I remember him saying he would like to have a child with me, so we would have the opportunity to raise a child together. That made me feel like there was a possibility I might have a girl after all. I remember joking with him about how he was going to propose to me. I was kidding around and laughing with him, but I was serious. I really did want to know what he was planning. I was cheated out of a "real" proposal with my first husband. This time, I knew Elvin was going to do something phenomenal.

I had been celibate for over three years. After I divorced my husband, I made that commitment to God and myself. I wanted to get to know myself and God more intimately during that time. I had vowed to stay that way until Elvin and I got married.

As we spent more and more time together, the feelings, the conversation, and our intimacy for one another became even stronger and more intense. Our love for one another intensified quickly. Our attraction and connection to one another couldn't be explained. We knew each other's thoughts. I could look at him and know when something was wrong, or off, or just not right. And he could do the same with me.

Then one day, it happened. Elvin and I were sexually intimate. My three-year celibacy period had come to a guilty halt. Oh, no! What happens from here? Although Elvin gave me exactly what my body needed and wanted, the bigger issue was that we had sinned. We did what we knew we were not supposed to do. I had expressed to Elvin many times that we couldn't allow that to happen. What do we do now?

Afterwards, we said we wouldn't allow it to happen again. We acknowledged our mistake, and we decided we couldn't let it continue. However, there was another problem. We didn't stop placing ourselves in situations where us having sex was the outcome. We continued those same behaviors and activities, thinking we were strong enough to fight our urges. Every single time, we proved one another wrong. Time and time again, I expressed I felt badly about what we were doing. Elvin felt the same way. We would agree we would stop being intimate but failed to keep our word time after time.

One Sunday, while our Pastor was preaching, he said, "*sin can't be managed.*" It was all starting to make sense. Once sin begins, it takes hold of you. Your mind is no longer your own. It was as if I knew it was wrong, but I couldn't stop myself from continuing to do what I knew was wrong. I told myself time and time again I would put my foot down, both feet down. I would stop having sex with Elvin. Each time I said it, I failed. Why? Because sin can't be managed.

I had allowed myself to step outside of God's perfect will for my life. I was extremely upset about that. I couldn't fault Elvin. He was struggling with this as much as I was. On top of that, I was a grown woman, who took responsibility for her actions! I had let my guard down, and I couldn't find the strength to pick it up again. The sin continued even after I prayed every prayer I knew to pray. I loved Elvin, but my relationship with God was more important. I wholeheartedly knew God had given Elvin to me. God had blessed us. I didn't want this issue to interrupt our beautiful relationship with one another. And I didn't want our sin to separate either of us from God. Yet the cycle of falling into sin and regretting it later continued. I knew God wasn't pleased, but I couldn't get past my own selfish desires. Was it really worth it?

Elvin and I continued to give in to our sexual urges. Then something happened that we definitely didn't expect. Uh - Oh! This can't be happening! We're what? Pregnant? What the Pastor said kept reverberating throughout my heart and mind, "*sin can't be managed.*" This changes everything. What do we do now?

The consequences of our actions were upon us. We had to forgo an official wedding proposal and the beautiful Church wedding I had envisioned for the past few months. I was sad and upset with myself. I couldn't believe I had allowed this to happen! This was now a part of my story. Correction, a part of our story!

I tried to focus on the positives. We were about to bring a beautiful bundle of joy into this world. Maybe I was about to have the baby girl I always wanted, but it was bittersweet. But I would have loved for it to happen after we said our "I Do's." The proposal I had been so eagerly awaiting wasn't happening now. I was looking forward to seeing what ideas he had to propose to me. We were out of order, and we were about to have to rearrange things to make way for our new bundle of joy.

We had some serious adult situations at hand. I didn't have medical insurance because of my entrepreneurial journey. We had a huge pile of medical bills. So, to "fix" things, we made plans to get married. It was happening sooner rather than later! We knew marriage was a part of our journey, but we hadn't planned it to happen this soon.

I was having my prayers answered amid my disobedience. I knew I wanted to marry Elvin. But I hated how things were being rushed. We had been looking at rings before finding out that we were pregnant. I was with Elvin when he picked out my set. He wanted to make sure I loved it, and I did.

After we got my bridal set, we made a day of it. We spent the day with family. We went out to dinner. And of course, we took tons of pictures.

By this time, I was about five months pregnant. My belly was enormous. I was often exhausted, but I was loving it. My growing belly was the light that came out of the darkness. I was carrying our love child. It was well with my soul. Nothing had changed about my love for Elvin. If anything, it had increased as we journeyed through our current situation. Elvin took great care of me. He always made sure I was not only good physically, but mentally as well. Elvin and I prided ourselves on how well we communicated with each another. He knew me and was well aware of the moments when I was condemning myself. He always had the right words to help me get past those moments.

Not long after we picked out our wedding rings, we decided on a date. I was so excited to be marrying my Mr. Wonderful. I could feel the love. I could feel his love intensifying as he nurtured me through our pregnancy. I was certain that with God's help, Elvin and I could do anything and everything as long as we did it together.

There was purpose in our union, behind our timeless story, and in us becoming one in holy matrimony. Because we love and highly respect our Pastor, I informed him that Elvin and I were getting married in a small ceremony outside of church. He was understanding and sent us his well wishes and prayers.

We had decided on a small, private ceremony, where we could confess our love before God and become one. We selected our date and found a notary public to perform our wedding ceremony. By this time, we were six months pregnant. I got all dolled-up with the help of some friends and family members. Purple is my favorite color. I already had a purple gown that was stretchy, so it made the perfect wedding dress for me. My nails were done with a splash of purple. I was absolutely beautiful, big belly and all. Elvin even humored me by wearing a little purple. Of course, I absolutely enjoyed taking a ton of pictures on the day I became Mrs. Dorsey!

I had a C-section with my first bundle of joy, so this birth was also going to be by C-section. I was excited to choose our baby's birth date and selected December 29th. I didn't want to have the baby on Christmas or New Year's Day. We were about to find out what it would be like to raise a child together as a married couple.

The moment was upon us. I was so ready to see our new bundle of joy. I had carried this child for nine months. I had seen his entire foot pushing on my belly. How amazing it is to be a woman!

Elvin was everything I needed him to be on delivery day. I was huge and as slow as a snail and a sloth mixed together. If I asked, he was there without question. The time had come. We were in the operating room. I felt every tug and pull. Then our baby boy was born. I heard him cry for the first time, and thanked God for our perfect, beautiful and healthy baby.

In the days, months, and years to come, we would reflect on our relationship. There were a lot of things we could have done differently. One thing remains true… We are still loving, learning, laughing, growing, and evolving together. Our Timeless Love continues!

A Deeper Look…

There is always sunshine after the rain, even if we caused the storm. The final Mr. Wrong led me directly to my Mr. Wonderful. The same day that I let go of the fake social media relationship with Bobby, God did a miraculous thing. He allowed me and Elvin to cross paths and see the beauty each of us offered the other.

Clearly, this was a divine set up. Elvin and I had been going in and out of the same church doors for three months without noticing one another.

God didn't allow me to meet Elvin until I had removed Bobby from my heart and my life. When God knew I was sincere about letting go of Bobby, he revealed my Mr. Wonderful to me.

This was totally a God thing. God's timing was unexpected, but perfect as always. God had set me up just to bless me! It was delayed because I had some heart and head work to do to prepare me for my Mr. Wonderful. The relationship with Bobby turned out to be a catalyst in my growth and in the love story I share with Elvin every day. I am thankful to God that even though it was delayed; it wasn't denied! My blessing was there for three months, waiting for me. I am forever grateful God directed the steps of my Mr. Wonderful and led him to me.

Now, I understand why the other relationships had to end. The Lord was making room for my Mr. Wonderful. I often recall a conversation I had with the Holy Spirit one day, while singing *Falling in Love With Jesus*. I remember Him saying, "The same way you're falling in love with Me is the same way you will fall in love with your husband." I hid those words in my heart, and every once in a while, I reflect on that conversation and am amazed by what God did in and with my life.

Could it be that this shy girl, who felt overlooked and not so pretty, was being swept off her feet in her very own love story? No man could take credit for what was happening in my life. I had gone through a process. I had to be healed of past hurts. God had to show me who I am. Everything I went through was necessary for me to experience the love of a good man and loving family. God did not allow me to waste one ounce of the pain that re-directed and positioned me to live my best life, NOW.

Wait on God to send the right person into your life! He/She will love your flaws and all. Elvin's strengths covered my weaknesses and vice versa. It is amazing how God did that, but that's what makes Him God! He knows exactly who needs to be with whom and why they need to be together. There is purpose attached to every God-created relationship!

God sent me the man of my dreams. Elvin was showering me with all the attention I could handle. He adored me and our children! Elvin and

Javeon had a special bond that was developing right before my eyes. Moments like those really mattered to me, because Javeon didn't have the best relationship with his dad. Now, he was forming a bond that male children need from their fathers. God knew not only what I needed, but He had Javeon in mind as well. He paid close attention to every detail of my life and intentionally designed a love story with me and Javeon in mind, and I am forever grateful.

The premarital sex that resulted in our pregnancy caught us off guard, for sure. But let me tell you about the goodness of our God. He is mindful of us, even when we're doing wrong. He has good plans for us.

Before we got pregnant, Elvin and I went on a beach trip. On the trip, I made a somewhat ridiculous prayer request. I had asked God to "allow" me to sin just one last time. My plan was to beg for His forgiveness afterwards. I begged Him to allow us to have some fun, just one last time. I promised we would stop sinning when the trip was over.

What was I thinking? Did I think I could just turn off the temptation? Did I think we could just quit? Did I honestly believe God would honor my request? Yes, I did.

As crazy as it sounds, I believed God would honor my request. I thought that somehow, someway; I was going to muster up enough strength to stop having sex with Elvin after the trip. I planned to put my foot down and declare there would be no more sex until marriage. Just like that, I was going to make it happen.

Sadly, it didn't happen that way. After returning from our beach trip, my prayers continued to be in vain. I didn't keep my promise to God or myself. A short time later, we were pregnant.

A piece of me believed if I had kept my end of the bargain, we wouldn't have gotten pregnant. I find peace in knowing God doesn't make mistakes. God knew we would sin. God knew I would make a "special request" of Him. He knew I wouldn't keep my end of the bargain. Even in all of that, He never stopped loving me. *"But God commendeth his love toward us, in that, while we were yet sinners, Christ died for us."* Romans 5:8 KJV

I knew that God still loved me, but I was heavily condemning myself. I could only think about how God had blessed us with this amazing relationship. Then we had sinned against Him. We had gotten pregnant before marriage, while we were going to church every Wednesday and Sunday and serving in various ministries. How could I? Those thoughts plagued my mind, day after day. I felt so guilty.

My feelings of guilt and condemnation continued throughout my pregnancy and childbirth. This was my second pregnancy, but it was certainly different from my first experience. When I had Javeon, we were showered with love from beginning to end. The baby shower was amazing. Plus, we had a lot of visitors during our hospital stay and after we came home. With our new love child, we only had a few visitors at the hospital, one or two to be exact. And no one from our church family came to my baby shower. If I wasn't in love and happy with my family, I would have experienced the church hurt that tried to simmer just beneath the surface. I chose not to ponder on it any further because I don't know the why. All I know is that I have a wonderful and loving husband and two handsome sons. I celebrated that instead of dwelling on the other.

Not long after that, God directed me to the following scripture, *"There is, therefore now no condemnation to those who are in Christ Jesus, who do not walk according to the flesh, but according to the Spirit."* (Romans 8:1 NKJV) When I read those words, it helped me to understand that God doesn't condemn. Condemnation is man-made. God convicts. When we are wrong, He corrects us, and when we are outside of His perfect will for our lives, He convicts us. Why? Because He loves us and wants what's best for us. I know He wants the best for Elvin, our children, and myself. I understood correction would come. No matter what anyone had to say about the circumstances surrounding our child's birth, I know he is our perfect gift from God.

Everything that happened in the year prior to his birth taught me to trust and rely on God. I'm grateful God gave me Elvin. I could talk to him about the things that were bothering me. Elvin said God had told him he would have to guard my heart. This is another reason I know Elvin is my one true love. God has been talking to him about me from the very beginning. God was preparing him and me long before we knew we would share our Timeless Love.

As the days, months, and years pass us by, I learn and discover new things about myself as I grow in and with Elvin's unconditional love. I didn't know I could experience a love like as this! I don't feel like I deserve it, but I thank God for the man He created specifically for me. Elvin encourages me every day to become the woman God created me to be.

Elvin and I continuously work on creating an unbreakable bond and building a healthy, happy, and whole family. Our Timeless Love is ongoing, and it will never cease. Our marriage is Built to Overcome, and our Timeless Love continues!

Conclusion

Because of the hurtful relationships I experienced in my life, I had lost pieces of myself. My beautifully broken pieces have been mended together by the Master Architect, Jesus Christ. I had to learn how to trust God and open my heart to receive what He had for me. I did not have a loving and stable father-figure in my life, and it made it hard for me trust God. When I surrendered and allowed God to complete me, God directed my footsteps to the path He ordained for me to follow.

I didn't understand how much my purpose was connected to helping women discover themselves. God had talked to me about my calling after I became an entrepreneur. A big part of my purpose seemed to be built around women, especially women entrepreneurs. I didn't fully understand this connection. I was going to pursue this venture. I established connections with women from all walks of life and coordinated events. As time went on, I came to realize the big picture. God gave me a passion and a purpose to help women understand their worth and the importance of self-love. I wanted to empower women to create their best life.

After receiving this calling, I had to ask God why I was having such a hard time keeping healthy relationships with females. Relationships I had treasured for years were falling apart, so why was I being called into the women's ministry? Lord, how am I supposed to pour into the women at my events and workshops when my heart is hurting? It didn't make sense!

Then God helped me to understand that the enemy was fighting against my purpose. The enemy didn't want my purpose to be fulfilled on earth.

The enemy knew if I was set free from my bondage, I could lead other women along their journey to freedom. I had to be prepared to fight for my freedom and theirs. Thankfully, God had a plan long before the enemy had a plot. *"For I know the thoughts that I think toward you, says the Lord, thoughts of peace and not of evil, to give you a future and a hope."* Jeremiah 29:11 NKJV

I am resolved to keep believing God has good plans for me. I remain hopeful that I have true sisters in Christ along this journey. My sisters and I can join together and encourage each other. *We truly are better together.*

My journey is ongoing. My growth has been absolutely amazing since I surrendered and allowed God to work in me and through me. I had to walk through my journey of healing with Him. God's ways are always perfect! I had to allow Him to dream a bigger dream for me than I could ever imagine for myself.

I am Built to Overcome… We are Built to Overcome! God built us to overcome any obstacles placed before us when we partner with Him. You have victory in the One who created you and formed you perfectly in your mother's womb! (Psalms 139:13 NKJV)

About the Author

Pam Dorsey, wife, mother, sister, and friend, born and raised in Greenville, SC. Pam is a Self-Love Expert, Affirmations Specialist, and a Life Pursuer. Pam is a graduate of Southern Wesleyen University and is certified in Personal Identity Based Leadership from the Identity Dynamics Company. After many years of not loving herself, finding Self Love on her own Self Love Journey empowered her to live like never before and want to see all women do the same. She is an avid lover of the ocean and waterfalls. She thoroughly enjoys spending time with her family, trying out new restaurants and shopping.

Pam's life's journey has perfectly positioned her to walk out her life's purpose, which is to Inspire one Woman to Influence another Woman and together we can Impact the World. She has overcome years of negative self-esteem, lack of self-love, non-existent self-confidence, and self-sabotage. Pam is the CEO of Pam Dorsey Enterprises, LLC, a women's empowerment company. She is purposed, empowered, and equipped to influence women to walk in their Authentic Wholeness. Pam wants nothing more than to see all women Healthy, Healed, and Whole which is her ultimate goal. She wants you to enjoy becoming the Wholistic Woman that God created you to be. Pam is all about them Two Shades of Beauty, because when you're beautiful inside it automatically flows outside!

Pam wants every woman that reads this book to know that no matter the situation and circumstances, there is nothing you can't overcome. Keep God at the very core of your life and you too can OVERCOME! Please know that with every step that you take, God has prepared the way, walked the way, and HE is with you in every step that you take. Come out of the darkness, discover new parts for you to love, and walk into His marvelous light.

Pam would absolutely love to stay connected with you. She welcomes your thoughts, concerns, and feedback. Follow her on all social media platforms at @IAmPamDorsey and via email Pam@PamDorsey.com. Join her VIP list and find out more about her various events, products, and services at PamDorsey.com.

www.ingramcontent.com/pod-product-compliance
Lightning Source LLC
Chambersburg PA
CBHW071017120626
46546CB00003B/1130